Revised Edition

How to Be Happy and Have Fun Changing the World

Written by:
Michael Anthony
www.howtobehappy.org

Cover design donated by:
Cherrie St Germain
Better Day Movement

Disclaimer

This book is not designed to provide psychological advice or to substitute for professional counsel. Its purpose is to increase your happiness by making you aware of the consequences of all your thoughts and actions. No responsibility is accepted for use of this information. Use is entirely at your own risk. Information contained is for educational purposes only.

Dedication

*My Happy Book is dedicated to
a very special spirit and dear friend,*

*Linda Harper
(11/2/1952 - 8/30/2006)*

who taught me much by her example.

*She was as hard as a rock,
yet as gentle as new fallen snow.*

Acknowledgements

Thanks to my mother and father for giving me the gift of life and the positive values they taught me as a child.

Special thanks to my mentor Philosopher Edgar Phillips for teaching me his profound insights into the chemical brain. Also, thanks to his wife, Helen, for generously giving me permission and her blessings to use the concepts and insights from his book, *Breakthrough*. Unfortunately, Edgar Phillips is no longer with us to see his ideas and philosophies blossom and bear fruit.

This is to thank you, if you decide to have fun changing the world one person at a time by starting with yourself and spreading the word.

Last, but not least, thanks to my hero Don Quixote for inspiring me to keep striving to help achieve the impossible dream of peace and harmony for all of us.

"How To Be Happy and Have Fun Changing the World"

Table of Contents

"How To Be Happy and Have Fun Changing the World"

Foreword

Michael Anthony has written a book about how to be happy. At first I thought, oh, no…not another self-help book. However, the idea of being 'happy' appeals to me, so I gave the short, 87-page manuscript my undivided attention. When finished, I closed the book and knew this profound (yet simple) message had the potential to improve lives – millions of them!

After you read this book, you'll never again look to possessions, people and things outside of yourself to make you happy. Understanding eight simple words will allow YOU to generate your happiness from within. You will realize that your happiness will never cost any money and no one can ever take it away from you.

Michael shows us that, contrary to popular belief, examining our negative emotions and sitting with them for a bit is actually a good thing. Once you comprehend the profound influence negative emotions have on you, you'll appreciate the rewards that are possible when you focus on releasing them – not just covering them up. It's simple if you focus on the eight words.

Surprise, surprise! The key to happiness has nothing to do with the acquisition of possessions, wealth or fame. By incorporating Michael's simple message into your life, your natural abilities will be revealed and then gain strength when you align your thoughts and actions with eight little words. You'll be more productive and creative…success follows. Money, a mere byproduct of success, will then enable you to afford those 'external' pleasures.

How to Be Happy and Have Fun Changing the World is an owner's manual for human beings. In a world where truth seems to be the exception, convenience the norm and blind ambition and greed rewarded, I find joy in the idea that 'being good' is a source of contentment.

I am thankful that Michael took the time to assemble an insightful group of words that reveal the basic concepts, which allow people to live a very happy life. His words will change your life as they have already changed mine. Read the book and you'll understand the magic and unravel the mystery.

At Better Day Movement we hope by sponsoring Michael's work and sharing his message with you, your life is happier and more meaningful. If enough individuals use these simple, yet profound insights, our world will change for the better.

Cherrie St Germain
Co-Founder
My TruMind / Better Day Movement

"I am only one, but I am one.
I cannot do everything, but I can do something.
And I will not let what I cannot do interfere with what I can do."

~ Edward Everett Hale

Chapter 1

The Introduction

If you are reading this book, you may have a couple questions running through your mind about me. Why did I write *How to be Happy and Have Fun Changing the World?* Will this book be able to deliver the goods or am I just a dreamer?

After writing *How To Be Happy*, I gave the valuable insights contained in this book away for free for six years from my happy website? My friends thought I was insane to do this. I'll tell you why I started charging for it towards the end of this chapter. I'm happy to report that my happy book has been widely read, and changed thousands of lives in many wonderful ways.

I wrote this book for several reasons. The first one is because I love sharing the insights contained in this book with others and it makes me very happy. The second one is because I wanted to reach a mass audience by addressing a subject that would appeal to most, if not all, of the people living on our planet. After all who doesn't desire to be happy or happier and make our world a better place for themselves, their children and their children's children?

The third reason is because I needed a feedback mechanism that you can easily relate to and cannot deny. Everyone knows whether they are happy or unhappy. You can decide for yourself what gives you true and lasting happiness. You will be able to judge for yourself if what I share with you makes total sense.

The most important reason is that this book allows me to introduce you to **Eight Words** that will help you increase your self-awareness and happiness. These **Eight Words** will help you make better choices that will change you and the world for the better, in the process. If you want to be happier and remain happy, this book will show you the way.

If you can honestly say that you're totally happy with all aspects of your life, are you happy with what is going on in the world? Unless you never follow the local news and world affairs, or live in a cave in the Himalayas, you're probably not happy about something or at least would like to improve it if you knew an effective way to bring about positive change.

I acknowledge that there are many positive things about our world, but you have to admit that some things could be much better. I'm not going to go into a commentary about what's wrong with the world; you can decide that for yourself. I wrote this book to increase *your* self-awareness and give *you* some positive steps to take, if you desire to be happier and have fun helping to change the world for the better.

By the time you finish reading this book, you will know if I'm a dreamer or a man with a plan that will work if *you* help out by doing *your part.* In the meantime, here is a very brief story of my life to help you get to know me better.

When I wrote *How To Be Happy* in 2005, I was in my early sixties. So I had some life experience to draw on. I was born in 1943 to a very religious blue-collar family. We didn't have much money, but I was given very solid values. I had a very happy childhood playing on the railroad tracks and swimming in the Baltimore harbor. Some would consider my playground dangerous, but to me it was lots of fun and adventure, Huckleberry Finn style.

After high school, I worked for two years to earn enough money to pay for my first year of college. Working part-time jobs during college paid for the rest. I was one of the rare kids in my neighborhood that went to college instead of going to work on the waterfront, or in the local factories like their fathers.

I majored in business and economics at the University of Maryland and graduated in three and a half years. I had a great time during my college years, and even became President of my fraternity Sigma Pi. My only regret was not taking the full four years to graduate.

From there I went to New York City and worked in the Wall Street area as an international banker for one of the largest banks in the world. In the evenings I worked on getting my MBA at New York University. I even got married to a wonderful woman. In the so-called "real world" I was making a lot of progress, but I realized that I wasn't having much fun anymore in my world.

The child in me was growing up and becoming unhappier day by day. By the time I was in my middle to late twenties, my ambition had dried up. I started to search for what would make me happy again. I looked into the future and realized that the outside world of riches and material comfort had little to offer me as a means to achieve true and lasting happiness.

I started reading books on philosophy and metaphysics. Blessed with a strong and ambitious spirit, I read lots and lots of these books. My inner world was coming alive again and my relationship with the "real world" outside was coming to an end.

My promising career in international banking came to a close. In my early thirties I moved to San Francisco. Eventually, I got a friendly divorce and kept searching for the answer to what would make me happy. My former wife and I are still the best of friends.

During this period of soul searching to find the answer of how to be happy, I would take high commission sales jobs with the hopes of making a million dollars so I could be financially independent and quit working. But, my spirit was restless and wanted me to keep searching for happiness. So I did. In hindsight, I probably would have made my millions if I loved what I was doing and stuck with any one of the several opportunities that I left behind. However, I'm glad that I kept searching.

It wasn't because I lacked discipline. I lacked direction. I had enough self-discipline to swim a mile or two in the frigid waters of the San Francisco Bay almost everyday for five years. I'm pleased to let you know that I swam across the span of the Golden Gate Bridge four times and from Alcatraz to San Francisco twice. I had plenty of self-discipline.

In my late thirties I met my mentor Edgar Phillips who taught me the secret to happiness, which I will share with you in this book. Armed with this knowledge, we tried to take it to the business world through a program designed to increase productivity in the workplace.

Unfortunately, during the early 1980's the business world had a hard time accepting the major principle of Edgar Phillips' philosophy. Can you imagine that the business world didn't readily accept being 100% truthful, *no matter what the consequences?*

I found out that business at that time had a hard time relating to the concept that being totally ethical would increase productivity. There was some interest, but I did not find any serious players in the business world that were open to what I had to share.

Since I'm not easily discouraged, I found success sharing this information with athletes because I related it to a feedback mechanism that they could not deny. I tied performance to the mind/body connection and it worked like a charm. In 1984 I moved to Los Angeles to be near the Olympics.

There, I met Ruby Fox. Ruby was struggling at the 1984 Olympic trials and had one last chance to make the U.S. Olympic pistol team. After only one forty-five minute mental training consultation with me, she shot 299 out of a possible 300 score and made the Olympic team.

During the Olympics, Ruby got into a sudden death shoot off for the Gold Medal. She ended up with the Silver Medal because she became giddy after a long string of perfect scores during the shoot off, and lost her focus. Afterwards, Ruby told me that she was very happy with her Silver Medal and it was an experience she will never forget.

In 1987 two-time world champion Lynne Jewell asked me to help her and her partner Allison Jolley to prepare mentally for the 1988 Olympics in Seoul, Korea. I did and they won the Gold Medal in yachting.

During the 1990's I fine-tuned my mental training program by working with golfers. I helped many golfers for free and supported myself with part time sales jobs when they were available because I was very good at selling products and services that I believed in.

There were times when I would sleep in my car or wherever I could to make ends meet. You couldn't pay me enough money to keep me from doing what I loved, even though I was not being paid. At times, I was forced to stop and regroup.

I've had many adventures -- and misadventures -- that I could share with you, but I'll leave that for a future book. Indeed, I was a **Man with a Mission** that could be slowed down, but not stopped.

Eventually, I did start charging for my one-on-one mental training consultations, and I trained well over half of the head PGA golf teaching professionals in Palm Springs. I wrote and self-published the book *The Mental Keys to Improve Your Golf* and began selling it on the internet from my website, mentalkeys.com, in 1999.

In 2004, I produced a CD, *Using the Mental Keys to Polish the Wheel*, which has been very well received as a complimentary addition to my book. If you are curious about what golfers have to say about *The Mental Keys* book and CD, visit my golf website and read the numerous testimonials from golfers at every age and skill level, raving about their lower golf scores as well as how its insights have improved their lives.

This holds true for my book *How To Be Happy and Have Fun Changing the World* as well. I am happy to report that during the six years when I gave this book away for free from my happy website, I received hundreds of emails from grateful individuals telling me how much my happy book has enhanced their lives in many wonderful ways. I receive so many positive comments that I rarely add the new ones to my website because there are already too many to read ☺. However, keep emailing them because I appreciate receiving your positive feedback.

In 2011, I expanded my distribution network by charging for my happy book's valuable insights that have the power to change your life as well as our world if enough individuals live by the **Eight Words** revealed in *How To Be Happy*. Hopefully, the increased exposure through major book distributors and the proceeds from my happy book will allow me to advertise and promote it on a much larger scale than in the past in order to help many more people, and eventually reach a critical mass with your help. You can help out by posting your comments about how much you liked this book on Amazon and other outlets.

I know that you will benefit from what I'll be sharing with you, and many readers will tell their family and friends about *How to Be Happy and Have Fun Changing the World*. They, in turn, will do the same.

Once a critical mass is reached, the **Eight Words** in my happy book will have a positive influence on many lives, and our planet's values. By the time you finish reading this book, you will understand how the power of these **Eight Words** can help change your life, and the world's values.

It may have taken me a while to get here, but I'm a very happy person and my spirit is having fun again. Now, it's my turn to help *you* and many others by revealing what has made me very happy. I hope you enjoy my book and tell your family, friends, and associates to read it as well.

Now that you know where I'm coming from, keep an open mind while reading the rest of this book. The proof is in the pudding.

"The Joy of Life"

This is the true joy of life. The being used for a purpose recognized by yourself as a mighty one. The being a force of nature instead of a feverish and selfish clod of ailments and grieving senses complaining that the world will not devote itself to making you happy.

I am of the opinion that my life belongs to the whole community and that as long as I live it is my privilege to do for it whatever I can. I want to be thoroughly used up when I die. For the harder I work, the more I live.

I rejoice in life for its own sake. Life is no brief candle to me. It is a sort of splendid torch which I have got to hold up for the moment, and I want to make it burn as brightly as possible before handing it on to future generations.

~ George Bernard Shaw

"How To Be Happy and Have Fun Changing the World"

Chapter 2

Owner's Manual for Human Beings

When I was growing up, my parents didn't give me an *Owner's Manual for Human Beings*. How about you? Were you given an owner's manual explaining how you were designed to function? Did it come with instructions how to operate correctly and happily?

My mentor's explanation of the chemical brain and how the brain processed information, along with his total commitment to the truth, *no matter what the consequences*, was an owner's manual that made sense to me. Edgar Phillips gave me direction and started me on the road to happiness. Reading about the insights of other great teachers and thinkers helped me to fine-tune this owner's manual that I'm about to share with you.

Human beings were designed by the Creator to all function the same way. A good analogy is the hardware of a computer. We are all hard-wired the same. What makes us behave differently from each other is the way we think, feel and act, which is our software.

What most individuals don't realize is that the power of your brain or computer's hardware varies according to the chemistry of your brain. You can dramatically increase the power and efficiency of your brain or personal computer by optimizing the chemistry of its cranial fluid. Let's take it step by step.

Improve Your Brain's Chemistry

It is critical to conceptually understand that your brain actually secretes chemicals corresponding to your positive and negative thoughts. The resulting chemistry of your brain's cranial fluid influences all of your natural abilities and functions. This, in turn, determines how well you perform in everything you do because your brain is like a powerful computer.

The power and efficiency of your wonderful personal computer can be increased dramatically by optimizing the chemistry of your brain's cranial fluid. This fact is very easy to demonstrate in the world of sports with athletic performance because of the mind/body connection. I have proven this to be true many times in the arena of athletic competition.

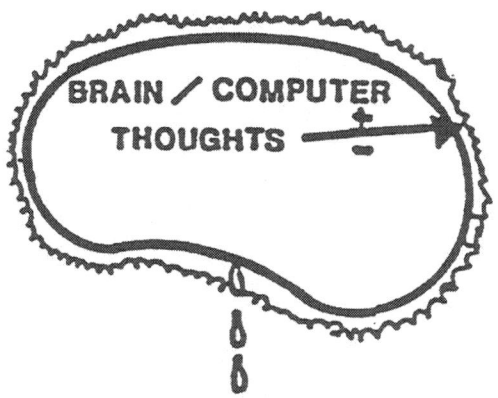

I am not going to explain the specific details of your electrochemical nervous system and list the numerous biochemicals that affect your behavior and performance. This book takes a common sense approach to a very profound conceptual explanation of what makes you tick as a human being. The details are not that important. The concepts are!

For example, do you know the chemical composition of the gasoline that powers your automobile or how the engine in your car works? You know that if you turn on the key and step on the gas pedal, your car runs. If not, you take it to a mechanic to have it fixed. You know that if you put water in the gas tank, your car will not run. It is not necessary for you to become a chemist or a mechanic to drive your car, as long as you understand the basic principles. It may be nice to know the details, but unless you want to be a chemist or a mechanic is it worth the time to learn?

The same is true of your electrochemical nervous system. It may be interesting to know the details. However, do you really have the time or desire to get a Ph.D. in neurobiochemistry, like Doctor Michael Raleigh at the Department of Psychiatry and Biobehavioral Sciences at UCLA School of Medicine in Los Angeles, CA? Doctor Raleigh specializes in the neurotransmitter serotonin.

While he experiments primarily with monkeys, he has done tests with athletes and fraternity members at UCLA. His research supports the findings that higher levels of serotonin in the blood correlate to higher performance levels and changes in behavior cause serotonin levels to change. I had the opportunity to meet with him in 1984 while I was in Los Angeles for the Olympics. He agreed that my owner's manual made sense and I was going in the right direction.

If you want an eye opening account of how positive emotions cause chemical changes that help heal the body, read esteemed endocrinologist Dr. Deepak Chopra's *Quantum Healing* (Bantam Books, 1989).

Your mind and body function together. Athletes live and die by the performance of their bodies. From their own personal experiences, they easily relate to the concept that their negative thoughts cause their brain to secrete chemicals that immediately impair their performance. This awareness helps them to be more objective and positive when dealing with challenges. It helps them to control their emotions and increase their performance.

A good metaphor to help you understand the influence of your brain's chemistry on your performance is a fine-tuned racing engine. Those engines, designed to run on super high-octane gasoline, sputter when using regular gasoline.

This is similar to what happens when you are negative. You put low- octane chemicals in your brain, causing your performance to suffer. When you are positive and operating on instinct, your brain, metaphorically, secretes super high-octane chemicals and your ability to perform excels as you enter the "zone."

Your brain receives input through your five senses.

SENSE STIMULI
See
Hear
Feel
Taste
Smell

Whenever you 'see', 'hear', 'feel', 'taste', and 'smell' something (stimuli), it enters your nervous system as an electrical impulse through a neuron (nerve cell). Once the electrical message reaches the end of the neuron (called a synapse) the electrical impulse/message converts into a biochemical (called a neurotransmitter). Then, this chemical message is converted back into an electrical impulse/message when it reaches the next neuron. This process repeats itself over and over until the message reaches the brain and is acted upon.

ELECTROCHEMICAL MESSAGES

ELECTROMAGNETIC FIELD

In reality you have an electrochemical nervous system. As the chemicals change, the messages change and your brain's performance varies accordingly. When you are positive and operating on instinct, your brain, metaphorically, runs on super high-octane chemicals. Your performance excels and you feel at your best.

20

It is important to realize that your electrochemical nervous system is an alternating electrical current that generates an electromagnetic field, which is infinite in nature. The strength and quality of your electromagnetic field is felt by those around you. As your awareness increases you will realize that you can't hide your feelings from those you interact with and they can't hide theirs from you. That's why you have good chemistry with people you enjoy being with and bad chemistry with those that you don't.

What is even more important to realize is that the electromagnetic field that your thoughts create cause attractor fields, which affect your life and happiness. We will talk more about the importance and power of the electromagnetic fields your thoughts generate in this chapter and in Chapter 6: Cause and Effect -- Attractor Fields.

You can increase your natural abilities and happiness by consciously adjusting the chemistry of your brain's cranial fluid. This fluid is affected by your thoughts, diet/nutrition, exercise, rest, environment and physiology.

THOUGHTS: As previously discussed, your positive and negative thoughts cause your brain to secrete chemicals. These chemicals, in turn, affect all your natural abilities and functions. Your thoughts have two components: facts and emotions. Every stimulus you receive through your nervous system is nothing more than a fact. However, you attach emotions to these facts.

It is imperative for you to realize that negative emotions cause adverse chemical secretions and hinder your natural abilities. Increase your awareness of the profound influence negative emotions have on your brain's chemistry, performance and happiness. Become more objective and restructure any negative emotional attachment you have to certain facts. Facts are merely facts. However, you can choose your emotional response to them. I'll tell you how as this book progresses.

DIET/NUTRITION: Everything you eat and drink is a chemical, which affects your performance and how you feel. If you doubt this, observe how a person's behavior changes when they drink some alcohol. Better yet, ask them how they feel the next day if they drank too much ☺.

Since there are many good books available on nutrition, I will just briefly touch on this subject. In the early cave dwelling days there were no factories and no processed foods. Humans are designed to live on natural foods with the proper amounts of protein, carbohydrates and fat.

I advise you to eat wisely and in moderation. Also, do not become neurotic about what you eat. Your emotional state is far more important than what you eat, even though what you eat is important.

EXERCISE: When I work with a boxer, swimmer, runner or any athlete who has to push himself to higher levels of physical exertion, I can normally skip this section. His or her daily training routine already includes several hours of intense physical conditioning. However, outside the world of sports, most individuals are out of shape. How about you?

In the early days of time, humans engaged in many forms of physical activity just to survive. Your body is designed to function properly with physical exertion so it can remove toxins and secrete beneficial chemicals. If you do not believe this, exercise the next time you are depressed. Notice how much better you feel after exercising.

For your body and mind to function at their best, it is important to exercise to make up for the lack of physical activity resulting from today's modern conveniences. Is 20 minutes of aerobic exercise three times a week too great a price to pay for a healthy body and an alert mental state?

When I lived in Palm Springs, I swam a mile almost every day. One day while I was showering after a swim, another swimmer remarked to me how much better he always felt after swimming. Then he added, "It is not like golf, which makes me feel worse after playing a bad round."

REST: Sufficient rest is necessary for the body to eliminate toxins and rejuvenate itself. Have you ever noticed that you sleep more when depressed than when you are excited and happy to be alive?

While you sleep, your brain is busy processing all the information it received during the day so that it can make spontaneous decisions when you're awake. This will be covered in greater detail when I explain *"Changing Your Tape"* later in this chapter.

ENVIRONMENT: When I refer to environment, I'm not just talking about the air you breathe and your physical surroundings. I am more concerned with the people around you. The electromagnetic fields they generate, as well as their thoughts and actions, can adversely affect you.

I strongly recommend associating only with positive people, or keep to yourself. The only time you should associate with negative people is when you are trying to help them. Your stronger electromagnetic field and positive thoughts and actions will have a positive effect on them.

Researchers have found that emotions, positive and negative alike, are nearly as contagious as colds and flu. You can catch feelings of elation, euphoria, sadness and more from friends, family, colleagues, even strangers. Mood "infection" happens in milliseconds, says Elaine Hatfield, a psychology professor at the University of Hawaii in Honolulu and a co-author of *Emotional Contagion* (Cambridge University Press, 1994).

When interacting with a negative person, take extra steps to remain positive. Otherwise, you may be influenced by his or her negativity.

PHYSIOLOGY: Your body reflects your emotional state. When you are positive and confident, you stand erect with your chest out and a smile on your face. If you just won $10,000,000 in the lottery, imagine how you would feel and how your physiology would respond ☺. You would feel on top of the world. Everyone watching you will see it by the way you carry yourself.

Imagine how you would feel and look if you lost your winning lottery ticket ☹. If this depressed you, your eyes would be down and your shoulders slumped. Some individuals would probably feel like killing themselves for losing their winning ticket.

Your physiology works both ways. Your body reflects your feelings. However, how you carry your body affects your feelings. One of the quickest and easiest ways to improve your chemistry is to change your physiology. By taking slow deep breaths, standing tall and sticking your chest out, you automatically increase your chemistry and immediately feel better. Raise your eyes to the sky and smile right now. Do you feel a change in your energy and alertness? If you always carry yourself like a winner, you will feel like a winner.

Your thoughts, diet/nutrition, exercise, rest, environment and physiology have a positive or negative impact on your brain's chemistry, which affects how well you perform and feel. To become happier and more successful, part of the process is to consciously work on increasing the chemistry of your cranial fluid so your brain can perform more efficiently and at higher levels.

Since your thoughts have the biggest impact on the brain's chemistry, that's where I'm going to focus in this book. When you have positive thoughts, your brain secretes positive chemicals and increases the power of your brain. When you have negative thoughts, your brain secretes negative chemicals and decreases the power of your brain. This is a simple, but profound concept to realize. Your happiness depends on it.

In the world of sports, this is very easy to demonstrate because the mind/body connection provides you with immediate feedback. When you are positive, your performance excels. When you are negative, your performance is adversely affected. My book, *The Mental Keys to Improve Your Golf,* explains this in great detail in relation to golf. This same understanding applies to your entire life.

However, when it comes to your personal, social and business behavior, the feedback may not be as obvious or as immediate. It may take you days, weeks, months or even years, to see or feel the repercussions from your negative thoughts and actions. I'm sure that if you reflect on your life, you will know exactly what I'm talking about.

Since you know the story of your life better than I do, I'm going to let you provide your own personal experiences and stories of how positive and negative emotions affect your happiness. Don't confuse short term pleasures from external sources with happiness. True and lasting happiness always comes from within. External pleasures never last.

Your thoughts from outside stimuli have two components: facts and emotions. While you may not be able to control the facts you encounter in your life, you can choose how to respond emotionally to these facts. If you choose positive emotions, you will be happy. If you choose negative emotions, you will become unhappy. Your happiness depends on what emotions you choose to experience and how you live your life. Your own life experiences will prove this to you if you are honest with yourself.

Let's take a quick look at the major positive and negative emotions. Anytime you have any degree of love, generosity, praise and bravery or multiple combinations of these emotions, your brain secretes positive chemicals and enhances your natural abilities. Positive emotions make you happy.

Anytime you have any degree of hate, greed, jealousy, and fear or multiple combinations of these emotions, you immediately lower your brain's chemistry and your ability to reason and function at a high level. Your negative emotions are the cause of most of your bad decisions, actions and unhappiness you experience in your life. The rest is caused by ignorance or lack of self-awareness. Stop and let this sink in.

Changing Your Tape

Let's take a look at why you think and act the way you do. Your brain starts working at a very early age. Approximately six months after conception, your brain starts recording all of your mother's thoughts and actions while you are in her womb.

Your brain continues recording all your thoughts and actions throughout your entire life. While you are reading this book, your brain is busy recording and comparing the information that I'm sharing with you to your past thoughts and actions. We will call the recording process of your brain – *your tape*.

Your tape is a conceptual representation of the entire history of all your previous thoughts and actions. The importance of your tape is that your brain or computer is programmed to make similar decisions according to what is in its data base (your past tape). On your tape is a record of all your positive and negative thoughts and actions that make up your life or comfort zone.

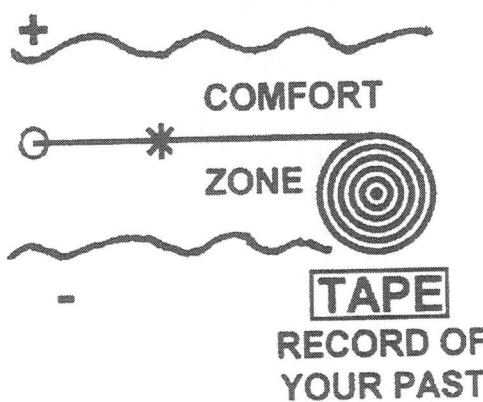

COMFORT

ZONE

TAPE

RECORD OF
YOUR PAST

Your brain spontaneously uses all of your strengths and weaknesses recorded on your tape in its decision making process. Your tape is programmed to keep you at your present level and within your comfort zone.

How you think and act today is merely a reflection of what is on your past tape or software. Most of your current beliefs were put on your tape by your parents and your social conditioning. The same holds true for your emotions.

Don Miguel Ruiz in his book *The Four Agreements* (Amber Allen Publishing, 1997) describes in great detail how your tape and everyone else's tapes are programmed by their parents and society. Reading his book will help you realize that many of your beliefs and thoughts on your tape are not your own. They were put there by others and you readily accept them as your own. Your present level of happiness is a reflection of what you have recorded on your tape. Our owner's manuals are very similar.

Since your brain is programmed to make decisions similar to what is on your tape, the biggest challenge you face when trying to change your past thoughts and actions to increase your happiness is your present thinking and belief system. Your level of self-awareness of what exactly is on your tape and understanding of how you were designed to function according to Universal and Natural Laws, greatly affects your ability to change and your current happiness.

In the next chapter, I'll show you how to increase your self-awareness so you will know what to change on your tape to increase your happiness. However, change is never easy.

When you try to change, you have to overcome what is on your tape. Your tape's job is to have you repeat what you have done in the past. Your job is to increase your desire and determination to change. Your tape does not care whether you are positive or negative. It is only concerned with having you repeat your past thoughts and actions.

I want you to completely understand that your tape is not your enemy. It is your friend. Without your tape, you would not have a memory. You would not know your name, who you are, how to talk or anything else that you have learned during your lifetime. Your tape provides you with your database for going through life. It's not your tape's fault that you and your social conditioning have allowed it to accumulate negative thoughts and actions that are holding you back and affecting your happiness.

Learn to be very honest with yourself. Find out what is on your tape. To reprogram your tape, you must increase your strengths and overcome your weaknesses. You are not going to change yourself overnight. It takes time, depending on the strength of your desire, and the positive actions you take to change.

If you decide to change, but repeat the same mistakes or negative behaviors, do not become depressed or beat yourself up. Instead, laugh at yourself. Acknowledge that your tape is strong and very good at what it does. After all, it knows everything about you. It uses all your weaknesses and excuses to keep you where you are. Learn to become comfortable with who you are and what is on your tape.

After you acknowledge that your tape has beaten you, decide who is in control -- *you or your tape*. There are some things your tape has total control over, since you may not presently be strong enough to change them. Do not become discouraged. Get more determined and work harder and smarter to change what you can. Eventually, you will acquire enough strength and wisdom to overcome your tape in the areas where it presently controls you. If you truly desire to be in control and implement the knowledge that I am sharing with you, it is just a matter of time and effort until you master your tape and increase your happiness.

Fortunately, you can change your past tendencies because the most current portion of your tape has the biggest impact on your decision making process. Otherwise, you would be a robot and never could change. Whenever you attempt to change anything on your tape, you face a *battle* between your desire to change and your tape's desire to do its job. The strength of your desire to change determines your success against your tape.

Many individuals in our society are overweight and out of condition. Most of them have a desire to change for the better, but their desire is too weak to overcome the strength of their tape. However, when faced with a life threatening heart attack or stroke, many of these individuals change their behavior. Their strong desire to live gives them the strength to overcome their past tape. They exercise, change their diet and lose weight.

Desiring to increase your happiness may not be a life or death decision for you. All I can say to you is that the greater your desire to increase your happiness, the greater will be your success. You do not have to go to the extremes that I did, but it certainly accelerates the process. The better you understand how your tape operates; what is holding you back; and how to implement change; the easier your journey becomes to higher levels of happiness and bliss. Your level of *desire* is one of the major keys to success.

When you go to sleep, your brain is busy processing all the thoughts and actions that went on your tape during the day. If you did something different from your normal routine, like exercising or dieting, your brain has to decide to either assimilate this as a new behavior, or reject it. Your brain needs to know how to respond in the future. By putting new thoughts and actions on your tape consistently for thirty days or more, your brain assimilates these as new habits. They become a part of your normal tape response.

The best times to give your tape goals or instructions on how to improve your behavior are just before going to sleep and when you wake up. While you sleep, your brain examines the goals or instructions that you just put on your tape. It has to make a decision how to respond when you wake up. It asks itself, "Whom do I believe, *the new you or the old you?"* The old you probably has been making similar goals or resolutions off and on for years, seldom carrying them out and behaving the same way for most of your life.

Your brain, more than likely, will believe the old you and instruct your tape to forget last night's goals or instructions. Your tape will go about business as usual. Therefore, immediately upon awakening reinforce your goals and put the instructions back on your tape. Remember, the most current portion of your tape has the biggest impact on your decision making process.

Assume you achieve your goals for several days in a row. For example, you actually do exercise or diet. Now, while you are sleeping, your brain starts to realize that it should begin listening to the new you. It begins to tell your tape to start responding accordingly and in about thirty days you develop a new habit. Then, your tape works for you, instead of against you. The more success you achieve, the easier it is to be even more successful because your tape becomes your ally. Now, it insists that you keep on improving. Your comfort zone expands to accommodate the new you as the old you drifts away.

As I mentioned above if you do something new or behave differently for thirty days, your tape will accept it as the new way to respond. However, if you give your tape an inch, it will go back to its old way of responding. That's why change is never easy.

Whenever you attempt to change anything on your tape, you face a battle between your desire to change and your tape's programming to keep you where you are. Your degree of self-awareness and the strength of your desire to change determine your success against your tape.

The time and effort you spend reducing the negative emotions and increasing the positive ones on your tape will determine how much you can increase your happiness. Wouldn't it be nice to be happy all of the time and live in a state of continual bliss?

Before I show you how to increase your self-awareness so you can make better choices and reprogram your tape to increase your happiness, let's review the key points of the *Owner's Manual for Human Beings*.

Key Points of Owner's Manual:

1) The power of your brain or your wonderful personal computer varies according to its chemistry.

2) Your brain's chemistry is affected by your thoughts, diet, exercise, rest, environment and physiology.

3) Your thoughts affect your electrochemical nervous system and generate electromagnetic fields that create attractor fields, which affect your life and happiness.

4) Your present thoughts and actions reflect what is recorded on your tape.

ır tape is programmed to repeat its past and does not
ıt to change.

6) Strong desire and proper direction are necessary to
change what is recorded on your tape.

7) Increasing your positive emotions and decreasing your
negative emotions will enhance your brain's chemistry
and natural abilities.

8) Increasing your self-awareness leads to better choices
that increase your chemistry and happiness.

Chapter 3

Self-Awareness and "The Eight Words"

Many individuals relate to having a spirit, mind and body even though they do not fully understand or comprehend it. However, most individuals believe that *they are their mind*, which is run by what is on their tape. This causes them to think that their mind or ego can make them happy.

Since it is impossible to describe what the spirit is in linear terms, you may find David Hawkins' explanation of the spirit, mind and body very insightful and helpful. For more information about David Hawkins, M.D., Ph.D. and his profound body of word, visit his website at veritaspub.com.

According to Hawkins the body cannot experience itself. You experience your body through your sensations. Your sensations in turn cannot experience themselves. Your sensations are experienced in your mind. Believe it or not your mind cannot experience its own thoughts and emotions. What is going on in your mind is experienced in your consciousness. Your consciousness is experienced in the Absolute.

Upon reflection, you will realize that there is a huge separation between your consciousness (spirit) and your mind. If you believe that you are your mind, and that your mind can make you happy, I highly recommend that you read Eckhart Tolle's wonderful book, *The Power of Now: A Guide to Spiritual Enlightenment* (New World Library 1999).

In this book, I am talking to your spirit and depending on your spirit to relate to what makes you happy. In my other book *The Mental Keys to Improve Your Golf*, I talk to golfers and depend on their mind/body connection to relate to improving their performance.

Since the mind/body connection does not lie, a golfer cannot deny that what I say makes total sense because the feedback is immediate and very obvious. Many golfers use *The Mental Keys* and see their scores quickly fall as a result of changing their negative emotions into positive ones. My reputation in the world of golf continues to grow as more and more golfers read my book, lower their scores and tell their friends. Helping golfers to lower their score is a piece of cake.

I have received many requests from my friends and other individuals that don't play golf to write another book for them. This is another reason why I wrote this book.

The challenge in writing this book is that outside the world of athletic performance, the feedback from your emotions may not be as obvious or as immediate. It may take you days, weeks, months or even years, to see or feel the repercussions from your negative thoughts and actions. However, be aware that it is just a matter of time until any negativity in your life eventually catches up with you and affects your happiness. There is a perfect accounting system in the universe. You can't hide or escape from it.

Since the negative emotions on your tape adversely affect your mind's ability to function and reason, it's a lot easier to relate to your spirit and not have to concern myself with trying to relate to what is on your tape.

If your tape is very positive, you will agree with the **Eight Words** that I'll be sharing with you shortly. These **Eight Words** will dramatically increase your awareness even if you don't live by them 100% at this time. If your tape is full of negative emotions, you will feel that it is impossible to live by the **Eight Words** 100% of the time in the so-called "real world."

Whether your tape is full of positive or negative emotions, your spirit will relate 100% to the **Eight Words** on the next page. I strongly recommend that you print out the next page with the **Eight Words** and put it in a nice frame where you will see it frequently every day like I do. Then, I challenge you to see if you can live by these **Eight Words** 100% of the time for 30 days.

Before I share the **Eight Words** with you, I want to acknowledge that you are already doing many things right in your life or else you wouldn't have achieved your present level of success and happiness. You have to admit, however, that we all have room for improvement.

Please read the **Eight Words** out loud to yourself three times and see how you feel. Then reflect on what the world would be like if everyone lived by these **Eight Words**.

"The Eight Words"

I
AM
ALWAYS
TRUTHFUL,
POSITIVE,
AND
HELPING
OTHERS

Can you even begin to imagine what the world would be like if everyone was *always truthful, positive and helping others*? Would it change the world we live in? You bet it would. It would probably come close to living in heaven on earth.

Is it possible for this to happen? Maybe not in our lifetime, but it can happen over time if everyone focused on living according to these **Eight Words**. Wouldn't a better world be a nice gift to leave to your children's children or their children's children?

Even if only a small percentage of our earth's population were always truthful, positive and helping others, our world would change for the better because the creativity and power of those that lived the **Eight Words** would overwhelm and positively influence those that weren't. The rest of the world's population would eventually follow out of their own self-interest to become happier and more successful.

The only question left to be answered is, "Are *you* going to be one of the leaders that help change our world for the better by living the **Eight Words** 100% of the time, or are you going to continue to live your life according to what is on *your tape?*" The negative emotions on your tape are limiting your ability to find creative solutions to your and our world's challenges. After all, our world's challenges are merely a reflection of the composite of the tapes of all the individuals that make up our global society.

If you doubt this, I invite you to read *Power vs. Force: The Hidden Determinants of Human Behavior* by David Hawkins, M.D., Ph.D. (Hay House, Inc 1995). In his book Dr. Hawkins presents a map of consciousness that explains why the power of one individual like Mahatma Gandhi was able to defeat the force of the entire British Empire through the principle of non-violence. Your spirit has enormous power at its disposal if you use it wisely. *You can make a difference if you choose to.* The **Eight Words** will help you to realize how.

Allow me to ask your spirit three questions. Are you always truthful 100% of the time? Are you always positive 100% of the time? How much of your time and energy do you spend helping others?

Pay close attention to your gut feelings or other changes in how your body feels when your spirit asks your mind or tape the same questions at the end of this paragraph. Because of the spirit/mind/body connection you will experience chemical changes in your body corresponding to your answers. When you tell the truth, you will feel strong. When you don't tell the truth, you will feel weak and sheepish.

Stop reading and ask yourself the following questions. Then pause and spend some time reflecting on your honest answers to these questions.

- Am I always truthful, 100% of the time?

- Am I always positive, 100% of the time?

- How much of my time and energy do I spend helping others?

If you answered 100% or came close to 100% to all three of these questions, you know exactly where I am coming from and you are without a doubt a very successful and happy person. If not, you have work to do that will increase your happiness.

I'm not there 100% yet, but I'm working on getting closer every day. If you desire to become happier and have an impact on changing your life and the world that we all live in, I invite you to make living by these **Eight Words** a major part of your life.

By the way, in reference to the above questions, who is doing the asking and who is doing the answering? Is it your mind talking to itself, or is it your spirit talking to your mind? Are you two different people in one?

The purpose of using these **Eight Words** is not to create angels. Its purpose is to create *self-awareness* by having your spirit guide your thoughts and actions throughout your life, instead of having your past tape continue to run your life for you.

Start saying the **Eight Words** out loud to yourself several times, or more, throughout the day for the next thirty days and watch your self-awareness increase as your spirit witnesses what is on your tape. Hopefully, you will use the **Eight Words** as your compass for the rest of your life.

Here is how the **Eight Words** will increase your self-awareness, and lead you to better choices that will increase your happiness. Your tape automatically has you repeat or make similar responses to what you have previously done. If you have lied in your past, your tape is programmed to have you lie again in the future unless you make a firm commitment to change your tape's programming.

I admit that I have lied in my past. If you are honest with yourself, you will admit that you have lied at least once in your life or maybe more often. By repeatedly telling your tape *"I am always truthful"* you create an internal conflict between your spirit and tape when faced with a choice of lying in the present or telling the truth.

You will experience this conflict as a chemical change in your body. You know what guilt feelings feel like, don't you? The **Eight Words** will make you very sensitive to your feelings, keep you honest and help you to do the right thing, in spite of what your tape wants you to do. It will make it harder for you to rationalize why it's OK to lie, especially when you see others around you that are not always truthful.

Your spirit will want to tell the truth, and your tape will want to do its job. Your tape wants you to repeat what you have done in the past. This gives your spirit a great opportunity to take a hard look at why you have lied in the past. It forces you to start realizing that you are your spirit, and not your mind. You have a choice, and do not have to automatically repeat what is on your tape even though your tape is programmed to have you repeat your past thoughts and actions.

If you examine your motives for lying, you will find them based on the emotions of hate, greed, jealousy, fear or multiple combinations of these negative emotions. By eliminating lies (including those little white ones) from your life, you keep negative emotions from recurring on your tape. This enhances your brain's chemical balance, and increases your awareness, sensitivity and intelligence.

Whatever level of truthfulness you have achieved in your lifetime, try raising your standards until you are 100% honest. I can honestly say that I am 100% truthful, most of the time ☺. As hard as I try to be 100% truthful, there are times when a reflex lie from my past tape slips by or tries to.

If I catch myself in a lie by feeling it in my body, I quickly take a look at why I lied, or why I am about to lie. Upon reviewing my tape I find that hate, greed, jealousy or fear is causing it. Then, I make the necessary adjustments in my life, and tell my tape to do my best never to lie again. Most of the time I'm successful in not allowing a reflex lie to slip by. You'll find this true for yourself if you start living by the **Eight Words** without exceptions.

You have the right of privacy and silence. If someone asks you a question and you want to reserve your privacy, you do not have to answer them. Become a diplomat and answer with another question or tell them that you prefer not to answer their question. Also, it is better not to upset or disturb another person's feelings or chemistry. You do not have to tell white lies to protect them. Instead, be kind and diplomatic in your response. Sometimes the truth, as harsh as it may be, is totally appropriate depending on the situation. Just make sure you intend to help the person, instead of venting any negativity on them.

Once your awareness and sensitivity to the chemical reactions in your body increase, you will realize the person you lie to the most is yourself. Every time you tell yourself that you are going to do something and do not do it or visa versa, you have lied to yourself and your tape. *Is it any wonder your tape just laughs at you when you say you are going to change your negative habits or emotions?* Your tape knows all of your strengths and weakness. It does its best to keep you where you are. It takes self-discipline and direction to become the master of your tape and in control of your happiness.

Two of the most important things that I have learned over the years are the power of self-discipline and the importance of making correct choices. Below are some of the late Napoleon Hill's thoughts on self-discipline from his book, *The Master-Key to Riches* published by Fawcett World Library in 1965 with the original copyright in 1945.

"Our Creator gave us all a free will to make our own choices. You are where you are and what you are because of your habits of thought. Your thought habits are subject to your control. *Self-discipline* is the principle by which you may voluntarily shape the patterns of thought to harmonize with your desires and goals. It is the one privilege, which determines more than all others the position in life you occupy. *Ponder this thought carefully for it is the key to your mental, physical and spiritual destiny.* Put your thought habits in order and they will carry you to the attainment of any desired goal you aspire to reach. You must feed your mind with your definite major purpose in life and go the extra mile to control all of your thoughts."

If you desire to be happier and more successful, your thought selection gives you the ability to shape and mold your life into whatever you desire. *Only your tape and wrong choices can hold you back.* With desire, self-discipline and the specific direction the **Eight Words** provide, you can become the master of your tape and destiny. More importantly, you can become very happy, and live a fulfilled life.

Your tape is going to continue doing whatever it is used to until it realizes that *you mean what you say.* If your tape controls you in a certain part of your life, acknowledge your weakness. Make a game plan to gain control in that area -- one day at a time. I'll show you how later.

By daily repeating to yourself that *"I am always truthful, positive"* your spirit will become very aware whenever you are or have been negative. This helps you to stop rationalizing and justifying the negative emotions that you have associated with certain facts on your tape.

Negative emotions poison your thinking and are the cause of much unhappiness. *It is a lot easier to become always truthful than to become always positive.* However, you will be much happier if you make it a point to do your best to be always truthful and always positive.

As I mentioned before, your thoughts from outside stimuli have two components: facts and emotions. Realize that facts are merely facts. You may not be able to control the facts, *fair or unfair*, but you can change or transform any negative emotional response you may have to them. I'll explain how as this book progresses.

By daily reflecting on *"I am always truthful, positive and helping others"*, you remind your spirit that by helping others you are helping yourself. By merely shifting your focus from yourself to helping others, you will find that you automatically feel better and happier. Your spirit is elevated when you help others.

If you are already very positive and in a position of comfort, lend a helping hand to those who are in need. One of life's greatest pleasures comes from helping others. If you do not believe this, ask any parent, coach, teacher or individual who spends his or her life helping others. What do you think Mother Teresa would have replied if you asked her, "Does it make you happy when you help others?"

If you really want to help someone, tell them about this book or give them a copy. Then, strongly recommend that they make living by the **Eight Words** a major part of their life. Better yet, be an example for them to follow by being truthful, positive and helpful to others 100% of the time.

The **Eight Words** are a wonderful compass that can help guide your spirit through the maze of life, *if you use them.*

If you truly desire to be happy and have fun helping to change your life and the world around you, reflect on the **Eight Words** at least three times a day, every day and observe how your gut or body feels. When necessary, make the appropriate adjustments on your tape in order not to repeat any deviations from these **Eight Words**.

I

AM

ALWAYS

TRUTHFUL,

POSITIVE,

AND

HELPING

OTHERS

Chapter 4

"To Thine Own Self Be True"

"This above all: to thine own self be true
And it must follow, as the night the day,
Thou canst not then be false to any man."

Shakespeare (Hamlet)

It's not my place to tell you that you do or don't live by the **Eight Words** 100% of the time. All I can do is strongly recommend that you be true to yourself when you reflect on these **Eight Words**:

I

AM

ALWAYS

TRUTHFUL,

POSITIVE,

AND

HELPING

OTHERS

You may be thinking about the classic story of Diogenes who went about ancient Greece searching for an honest man in vain. With over six billion people on our planet today, how many 100% honest people do you think Diogenes would find today?

If you can honestly say that you are 100% truthful and positive all of the time, I sincerely take my hat off to you because you are indeed an exceptional individual. If you are not 100% truthful, positive and helping others *and admit it*, I take my hat off to you because you are at least being true to yourself.

Without being true to yourself, the **Eight Words** will only be *eight hollow words* without meaning to you. *Empty words* will not increase your self-awareness and lead you to true and lasting happiness.

However, if you are true to yourself and make it a daily habit to repeatedly reflect on the **Eight Words** throughout the day, you will become very aware of what is on your tape and stop making choices that, sooner or later, lead to unhappiness.

Why did Thoreau in *Walden Pond* claim, "Most men lead lives of quiet desperation?" Was he making this up or is it true? For me it was true until I made it a priority to find what would make me truly happy.

Bare in mind that I was already a very positive and upbeat person before I started my search to find more meaning in my life. However, there was something missing inside of me. Fortunately, I was true to myself, admitted it and did something about it.

Living by the **Eight Words** made me realize that I was not my mind. I became aware that I was a spirit having a human experience. They helped me to reprogram my tape and transform my negative emotions into positive ones. They helped me to become very happy, and experience many moments of pure bliss. The best part is that my life keeps getting better and better.

If you are truly happy and full of bliss, stick around and listen to what I have to say. You may find that you can be even happier, and help others to be the same.

If you desire to live a happier and more meaningful life, start reflecting on the **Eight Words** to become aware of how much your past tape controls your life and why you do the things you do.

If you're not ready to be always truthful, become more truthful. If you're not ready to always be positive, become more positive. If you're not ready to always be helpful, become more helpful. Above all, to thine own self be true.

Life is a journey. It's a learning process. It has been said that success is the progressive realization of a worthwhile goal. Hopefully, you'll make living your life in accordance with the **Eight Words** 100% of the time your goal. If you do, you will make better choices as your awareness increases, and the happier you will become as you attract more and more positive situations into your life.

The **Eight Words** will guide you by limiting your choices to only those that are always truthful, positive and helping others. Your spirit will become very aware of the negative thoughts, actions, and emotions on your tape that are keeping you from experiencing true joy and bliss in your life.

The **Eight Words** will help you to reduce and eventually eliminate any lies or negative thoughts and actions from recurring on your tape. They will increase your positive thoughts and actions, which raises your chemistry and increases all of your natural abilities. Above all, they force you to be true to yourself and to your fellow man and woman.

If you are not willing to be true to yourself and use the **Eight Words** as your compass to guide you on your journey, you might as well save your time and pass on reading the rest of this book because it will only have a marginal impact on your life and happiness.

However, if you are willing to be true to yourself and make living by the **Eight Words** a major part of your life, keep reading because you will be amazed at how fulfilled and happy you can become. You will know the truth and the truth will set you free.

Man with his burning soul
Has but an hour of breath
To build a ship of Truth
In which his soul may
Sail on the sea of death
For death takes toll
Of beauty, courage, youth
Of all but Truth.

~ John Masefield

Chapter 5

External versus Internal Happiness

Have you ever reflected on why you do the things you do and what makes you happy? Once you have taken care of your basic needs of food, clothing and shelter for survival, you probably do things because they make you happy or keep you from becoming unhappy?

Since everyone has different thoughts, actions and emotions on their tape, I have to relate to you in general concepts instead of specifics. That's why it's so important for you to be true to yourself when you reflect on your own life and what I am sharing with you.

Take an honest look at your life and realize how much the different emotions on your tape affect your view of the world and happiness. You do the things you do because of what is on your past tape and your spirit's level of awareness.

Do you depend on possessions, people and things outside of yourself to make you happy? Do you depend on escapisms like watching television, movies or sports, playing games and taking external substances to make you happy or mask your unhappiness? If you do, you are looking for happiness outside of yourself.

The business and advertising worlds know this very well. They use your dependence on things outside of yourself that make you feel good, to entice you to buy what they are selling. Have you ever taken a serious look at why you buy the things you do?

You buy things and spend money on escapisms because they make you feel good. Don't get me wrong. There is nothing wrong with enjoying the world outside of you by having lots of possessions or escaping to relax.

However, don't expect the outside world to produce lasting happiness because after the initial euphoria wears off, you will find yourself looking outside of yourself for more, or different things to make you feel good again. It's a vicious cycle. The more you get, the more you need to maintain your happiness. You end up being a junkie dependent on things outside of yourself to make you happy

I could write an entire book on how you look to the outside world and escapisms to make yourself happy. However, it is better if you come to that realization yourself. Look around and reflect on all the things outside of yourself that you depend on to make you happy, or mask your unhappiness.

 Start observing all the advertisements that promise to increase your happiness, directly or indirectly, if you buy what they are trying to sell you. Pay attention to what you desire to buy in order to be happy or happier.

Are you buying or trying to buy your happiness? Are you are waiting for things in the future to make you happy? Do you tell yourself that "I'll be happy when I get _____ (fill in the blank)?"

I'm sure you have heard the expression that money can't buy you happiness. The reason this is true is because true and lasting happiness always comes from within. Yet, many individuals depend on things outside of themselves to make them happy. How about you?

If you want to reduce or eliminate your dependency on things outside of yourself to make you happy, structure your life so you can generate your excitement and happiness from within. The great thing about internal happiness is that it doesn't cost you any money to acquire it and no one, except yourself, can ever take it away from you.

How does one create internal happiness from within? It is very easy to do if you think about it. If you want to be happy, all you have to do is stop thinking about yourself and help others. The less you think about yourself and the more you help others, the happier you will become. This is a fact.

Why do I make this claim with such certainty? The reason is because your brain secretes positive chemicals corresponding to your positive emotions. When you help someone, you are being *generous* with your time and personal resources. You are being *brave* because you are not afraid of losing out while you are helping someone else, instead of yourself. Plus, you experience the feeling of *love* and well being when you help someone.

As a side benefit, these positive emotions elevate your chemistry, allowing your natural abilities to increase as well as your health. When I work with golfers and other athletes, I stress that they take time out of their busy schedules to help others because it will raise their chemistry and allow them to perform at higher levels in the competitive arena.

I'll offer you the same advice. Take time out of your life to help others because it will make you feel happy inside. Better yet, choose a vocation that you enjoy where you help others while you are earning your livelihood even if you make less money than you could earn doing something else. Invest your time and energy wisely because the more people you help, the happier you will feel.

Also, the more honest and positive you become; the less stress you will experience in your life. Do you know how great it makes you feel when you know that you always do the right thing and you are here to help others? If you don't know, I'll tell you. It puts a big smile on your face and makes your spirit glow inside. People can even see it in your eyes.

I'm sure some of you reading this chapter are rolling your eyes to the ceiling and shaking your head sideways. Your tape is telling you, "What nonsense" or, "I'd rather have lots of money and buy my happiness." Some tapes are saying, "If I'm always truthful, I won't make or have as much money to buy things that make me happy."

Some of you don't like what you do for a living, but resign yourself to putting up with your job as a means to buy things that will make you happy, or escape on the weekend. Your tape would rather have you work at something you don't enjoy because you can make more money than you could if you worked doing something you loved, but paid you less. That's what my tape told me until my spirit rebelled.

Maybe, this is what Thoreau was referring to when he said, "Most men lead lives of quiet desperation." If you love your work and make an honest living by helping others, you are a very rich person in many ways.

> *"Choose a job you love and you will never*
> *have to work a day in your life."*
> *-Confucius*

Have you ever heard the saying, "Do what you love and the money will come?" It took me a while to figure out how to do it, but I know from my own personal experience that this is true.

The popular motivational speaker, Zig Ziglar, has said, "You can get anything you want in life if you help enough other people get what they want." You can have the best of both your inner and outer worlds, as long as you are always truthful, positive and helping others.

The reason I say this is because the house always wins. Las Vegas, the gambling capital of the world, attracts millions of visitors a year and makes billions of dollars by playing the percentages. They make the rules and set the odds in their favor. You may win some money, but if you keep gambling in the hopes of winning more, you will end up losing because in the long run the house always wins.

What does Las Vegas have to do with this book and your happiness? It is just an example to illustrate that the house always wins. Let's take a look at you and the big picture of life.

If you were the Creator, the House in this example, who gave the seven billion individuals presently living on this planet a free will to do whatever they pleased, would you like to retain some element of control over your creation? It only seems logical that you would. But, how could you *control* these individuals and give them a *free will* at the same time?

If I were the Creator, I would design individuals with a free will to choose and do as they desire. However, I would set up a system of checks and balances to maintain control of my creation. I would do it by designing them so when they were truthful, positive and helping others, their brains would secrete beneficial chemicals. This would enhance their ability to think, perform and co-create in the direction that I wanted the universe to evolve.

When they were untruthful, negative, and selfish and going in the wrong direction from what I desired, their brains would secrete detrimental chemicals. This would hinder their thinking, health and performance, limiting the damage they could do to the positive evolution of my creation.

Think about it. With this system of checks and balances, the odds would be in my favor. Every individual would have a free will and I would have control of my creation. This is the system I would design and use if I were the Creator. Does this make sense to you? How does this make you feel?

If your spirit has evolved, this scenario probably makes a lot of sense to you. We were designed to function according to the laws of

God, or a Higher Power, or the Universe, or whatever Cosmic Intelligence or Infinite Source you feel comfortable calling It. If you are truthful, positive and helping others, you get rewarded. If you are untruthful, negative and selfish, you pay the price until you learn your lesson because the House always wins. It's just a matter of time.

If your tape feels that it is unrealistic to be always truthful, positive and helping others in the "real world," that's OK for now. However, when you find yourself unhappy, bored or depressed, take a look at why. Is it because you are depending on the world outside of yourself to make you happy? Is it because you are paying the price for being untruthful, negative or selfish?

If you depend on things outside of yourself to make you happy, the **Eight Words** will create conflicts with your tape. However, if you structure your life to live by the **Eight Words**, you will find that your internal happiness will grow and your dependence on things outside of yourself for your happiness will diminish.

However, as your natural abilities increase by aligning your thoughts and actions with the **Eight Words**, you will find yourself more productive and creative. More than likely, you will end up making more money and be able to afford more outside pleasures as well.

If you desire to have outside riches as well as internal happiness, do yourself a major favor and read the classic book *Think and Grow Rich* by Napoleon Hill, which was written in the 1930's. This book is still very popular because it shows you how to live by the House rules and achieve both outer and inner riches in abundance.

God gave you a free will to do as you please. You can look for happiness outside of yourself or choose to find happiness within by doing the right thing. Fortunately, you can have both if you play your cards right.

If you take care of the inside by playing by the House rules of always being truthful, positive and helping others, your outside world will take care of itself because you will have God on your side to help you out. Since God gave you a free will, the choice is yours.

If you want to read a great book full of commentary on how your spirit can be a co-creator with the Source of all creation and live a happier and richer life, read Dr. Wayne Dyer's *The Power of Intention* (Hay House, Inc. 2004). When you read *The Power of Intention*, pay close attention to how the **Eight Words** will align you with the Source of all creation if you live by them.

Chapter 6

Cause and Effect -- Attractor Fields

Since we live in a world of physical form and have a body, it is easy to see why you may view the world from the outside, instead of the inside. To help you understand how much your innermost thoughts affect your outside world and happiness, let's take a look at the law of cause and effect or attractor fields as Dr. Hawkins calls them in his book, *Power vs. Force.*

The law of cause and effect is based on the phenomenon that your thoughts are a cause and manifest themselves as physical forms or effects over time. In other words, if you want to go from **A** to **Z**, all that is required, is to focus and hold all your thoughts and actions on **Z** until they manifest themselves into physical form or effect.

This chapter presents two explanations as to how the law of cause and effect works. However, Hawkins states that cause and effect occur simultaneously in attractor fields in accordance with your consciousness.

The first explanation is based on modern scientific discoveries. The physical world we live in is made up of objects in many configurations whose building blocks are comprised of atoms.

These atoms are made of infinitesimally small positive, neutral and negative energized subatomic particles, whirling around at great speeds and great distances from each other in relation to their size. If you think about it, you will realize that there is much more empty space than solid matter in the physical objects that surround us, including the body you occupy.

If you look at the stars in the sky at night, they will resemble a picture of what the subatomic particles that make up your body look like. There is a lot of empty space between each star. Whether you realize it or not, the vastness between stars is similar to the empty space between the subatomic particles that comprise your body.

To a quantum physicist, **solid matter does not exist** as we know or perceive it. Atoms consist mainly of *empty* space! Since atoms continually exchange their subatomic particles with each other, there is a physical connection between all objects.

"We are all part of one inseparable web of interconnections and relationships of matter and energy" states actress Liv Ullmann in the insightful movie, *MindWalk,* based on physicist Ph.D. Fritjof Capra's book, *The Turning Point.*

At our present level of knowledge, physicists have identified only four forces that exist in the universe. They are the (1) strong and (2) weak forces of the atom, (3) gravity and (4) *electromagnetic fields*. These forces cause atoms to take their various shapes and forms.

Our electrochemical nervous system is an alternating electrical current that generates an *electromagnetic field* that is infinite in nature.

ELECTROCHEMICAL MESSAGES
STIMULI ➡ ⊖⋮⊖⋮ETC.
ELECTROMAGNETIC FIELD

Therefore, the quality and intensity of our daily thoughts (facts and emotions) generate *varying electromagnetic fields.* Consequently, our thoughts produce *one of the forces* that influence the atomic structure of the physical forms or objects that make up our so-called "real world." Our thoughts cause our physical world to take form according to the electromagnetic or attractor fields we create.

According to the law of cause and effect, we attract what we think about, both positive and negative. If you want to increase your happiness, use the **Eight Words** to choose your thoughts and emotions wisely.

New York Times best selling author Gregg Braden in his *Awakening the Power of a Modern God* (Nightingale Conant, 2004) explains that our outer world is a mirror of our inner thoughts. If you want to change your outer world, start by changing your inner world.

Another way to explain the law of cause and effect is to examine the nature of what we are. As I mentioned before, most individuals agree with the concept that they have a spirit, mind and body even though they do not fully understand or comprehend it.

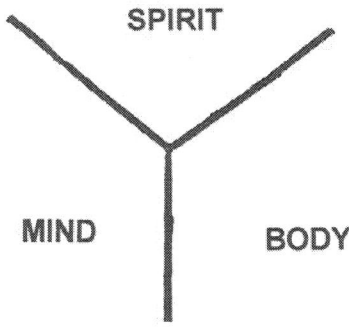

SPIRIT

MIND   BODY

Since your body has physical form, it is comprised of matter, which is limited by the dimensions of time and space. The scientific definition of time is the period it takes a body or object to move from one point in space to another.

Now ask yourself this question. Does your spirit have physical form? Think about this for a couple of minutes. *Does your spirit have physical form?*

To the best of my knowledge and that of the many individuals to whom I have asked that same question, your spirit *does not* have physical form. As a result, your spirit is not limited by the dimensions of time and space. Therefore, your spirit exists in the past, present and future and has no boundaries of space, time or knowledge.

What a paradox! *Your body has time and space limitations while your spirit or thoughts do not.* Stop and let this sink in. This ***time paradox*** can lead to conflict and confusion if you are not aware of its existence.

According to the law of cause and effect, your thoughts are a cause. Your thoughts cause your brain to secrete biochemicals that influence all your natural abilities and functions. They, also, influence the electromagnetic field that your electrochemical nervous system generates and initiate the law of cause and effect or attractor fields to manifest your thoughts into physical form or effect ***over time***.

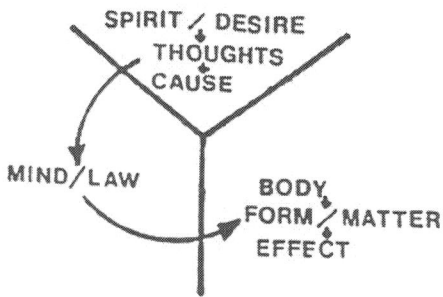

The reason our thoughts or desires seem not to manifest themselves is because of the ***time paradox***. Physical objects have limitations of time and space, while our thoughts do not. *Since it **takes time** for our thoughts to appear in the dimension of form,* we begin to fear and doubt that we will achieve our desires, or ever reach our goals. Next, we become frustrated or angry because it is taking too long or too much time for our desires or goals to be realized.

The negative emotions of fear and anger you experience before your desired goals take physical form create conflicting electromagnetic fields. In many cases, these negate the positive goals you desire and you end up manifesting your fears and frustrations, as well as any other negative thoughts you have. Your initial positive thoughts **A** about manifesting **Z** dissolve into a big question mark when you become negative in any degree.

A ⟶ ///// ⟶ ?

Since we are not alone in the universe, there are other causes with which we must contend, as I explained in the big picture of life. If your thoughts are out of line with the order of the universe or God's Will, guess who will win?

The Great Masters throughout the ages have taught that if you want to experience happiness and enlightenment, it is important to align your thoughts in harmony with God or the universe so you can use this Energy to work for you.

If your thoughts and actions are out of alignment with the Source of creation, the Source will work against you. It will eventually neutralize or destroy you unless you change your ways. Even Luke Skywalker in the movie *Star Wars* was told, "May the force be with you" and not to let his anger open him up to the dark side of the force.

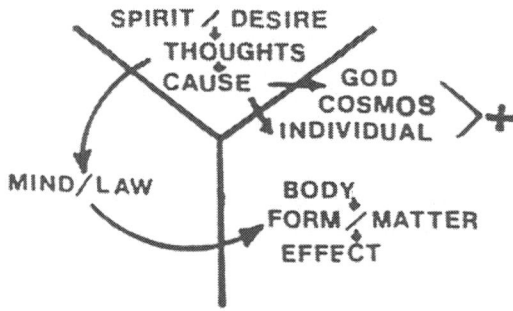

If you swim in the direction the river is flowing, its energy assists you. However, if you swim upstream against the river's flow, it is only a matter of time until you become exhausted and flow downstream with the river. If you want to know how you can tell if your thoughts are in harmony with God or the cosmos, ask yourself, "If I am always truthful, positive, and helping others, how far off can I be?"

You may be wondering "What have I gotten myself into by reading this book?" This book is a result of my desire to understand what life is about and how to be happy. Once I found some of the answers, it was only natural to want to share this understanding. I decided to make it practical and applicable to the "real world," so others could relate to it.

Because the mind/body connection cannot be denied, the solution was found in sports and helping athletes become more successful. My successful track record with athletes speaks for itself. Now I'm sharing this knowledge with you. Hopefully, *you* will put it to good use.

It has taken me many years to understand through my own personal experience that the law of cause and effect works, *but it works over time.* In spite of my expanding awareness, I am still subject to fears and frustrations, but they are becoming less and less as my awareness continues to grow. I know from my own personal experience that it is only a matter of time until my dreams come true, as long as I keep my thoughts positive and eliminate any negativity.

The **Eight Words** have helped many of my dreams to come true, and these same **Eight Words** will help you to make your dreams come true, if you use them to guide your life. My dream is to help you and eventually our world's population to become always truthful, positive and helping others. *You* are invited to share my dream, and help make it come true.

To increase your understanding of how you can use these Natural Laws, which govern all of creation, to increase your happiness, I recommend that you read New York Times best selling author Dr. Deepak Chopra's *The Seven Spiritual Laws of Success* (Amber-Allen, 1994). His powerful principles will help you to attract success and happiness in all areas of your life.

"How To Be Happy and Have Fun Changing the World"

Chapter 7

The Proof is in the Pudding

Depending on your level of self-awareness, you may be scratching your head at what I have shared with you so far. Or, you may know that what I'm sharing with you makes total sense from your own personal experiences and spiritual awareness, even if you don't live this way 100%.

The only way that you can validate what I'm telling you is true or not true is to experience it for yourself by being always truthful, positive and helping others. Then, observe the results. Since the proof is in the pudding, live your life in accordance with the **Eight Words** 100% of the time, and then experience the positive results in your life.

If the same information that I'm sharing with you has helped thousands of golfers to lower their scores and elite athletes to win medals in the Olympics, it's only logical to conclude that it will work for you in your daily life since our hardware is all the same. Remember, it's only your software – how you think that differentiates you from everyone else.

The only difference between you and an athlete is how long it takes you to experience or recognize the repercussions from being untruthful, negative and selfish. In the world of sports, the feedback is immediate and easy to see because negative emotions literally destroy an athlete's ability to perform at high levels. A smart athlete learns from his or her mistakes. Hopefully, you will too.

If you still think that you are your mind, reflecting on the **Eight Words** daily will force you to start witnessing how you behave according to what is on your tape. Your spirit will become the witness of all your thoughts, actions and emotions. Your spirit will know when you are living according to the **Eight Words**, and more importantly when you are not living according to the **Eight Words**.

Living by the **Eight Words** will help you to reprogram your tape, and increase your awareness and natural abilities. It will help you realize that you are not your mind, and your internal happiness is not dependent on the outside world. You will learn that the outside world is a reflection of your inner world, which you can control if you have a very strong desire and back it up with positive action.

If your mind is resisting making a total commitment to live 100% by the **Eight Words**, ask yourself why. Then, write down your reasons. Since I can only talk to you through this book, it is impossible for me to address each and every one of your personal reasons.

However, I can predict with 100% certainty that whatever reason your tape comes up with for not making the decision to live by the **Eight Words** as a major goal of your life, there will be a negative emotion attached to it. Otherwise, why would you resist committing to being always truthful, positive and helping others? Be aware that your negative emotions adversely affect your mind's ability to think, function and reason.

If you feel that you are already always truthful, positive and helping others, make it a point to see if you are being true to yourself. If you are the rare exception and are already living the **Eight Words** 100% of the time, feel free to skip this chapter and read Chapter 9: Have Fun Helping to Change the World.

If you have decided to live by the **Eight Words** 100% of the time or to the best of your ability until you can, here are some insights that have helped me to live this way and can help you to do the same. These are the same principles or mental keys that are explained in my book, *The Mental Keys to Improve Your Golf.*

These insights can be used to increase your success and happiness in everything you do in your life. However, the three prerequisites needed to benefit by these insights are *desire, honesty and an open mind.*

Desire

The first step in undertaking any journey begins with ***desire*** to reach a destination or goal. Without desire, you would not even get out of bed in the morning. The greater the journey to success and happiness, the greater the amount of desire required.

How much desire is required to reach your goals? The strength of desire needed is in direct proportion to the degree of success you wish to attain. If you desire to be the best in the world, you need to have the strongest desire. On the other hand, if you only want to be mediocre, you only need a mediocre desire.

On a scale of 1 to 10, 10 being the highest, your level of desire must be a ***10 plus*** if you expect to be the best at whatever you choose to accomplish.

DESIRE ➜ 10+

The following story will help you relate to what a desire of 10 plus is.

Once upon a time, a Zen student asked his master when he would reach enlightenment. The Zen master replied, "When your desire is strong enough, you will attain enlightenment." The frustrated student, who had spent years studying under the master, felt his desire was already sufficiently strong. The master, sensing this frustration, led his student to a pond to teach him a lesson on desire.

When they were waist high in the water, the master asked the student to kneel down. Then, the master held the student by the shoulders and submerged his head under the water. As the seconds without air became minutes, the student desperately needed to breathe. The student tried to raise his head above the water's surface. The master relentlessly kept his student's head firmly under the water.

After a great struggle, the student finally broke away from his master's steel grip and caught a breath of air. The student gasping for breath cried out at his master, "Are you trying to kill me?" The master sternly replied, "When your desire for enlightenment becomes as strong as your overwhelming desire to breathe was, you will find enlightenment."

When I started my search to find happiness and a more meaningful life, I had a very, very strong desire to find the answer. I wasn't looking to become enlightened, I just wanted to be happy and live a meaningful life. In the process of doing my very best to live by the **Eight Words** without exception, my self-awareness and understanding of the big picture of life has grown immensely and continues to grow.

Since we live in a very orderly universe, I found that we must limit our desires to stay within Natural and Universal Laws, or suffer the consequences that our misdirected desires create for us. Living in accordance with the **Eight Words** has helped me to eliminate many desires and distractions that were leaving me unfulfilled. I was confusing short term pleasures that did not last with inner happiness that did.

It takes a very strong desire and total commitment to be able to live by the **Eight Words** 100% of the time, otherwise your mind will rationalize why it's OK to make exceptions whenever it is convenient.

Goals: Outcome versus Process

Many individuals do not realize that there are two types of goals. There are *outcome goals* that give you direction, such as: being happy, having a good education, being married, having children, having a job you love, having money, owning a house, car, and etcetera. What are even more important are *process goals,* which include the dedication and hard work required to achieve your outcome goals.

Webster defines ***process*** as "a series of actions or operations conducing to an end." If you perform the process correctly, the outcome takes care of itself. If you want to be on the other side of the street (outcome), do the process of pointing yourself in the right direction and taking one step at a time until you reach the other side of the street.

Living the **Eight Words** is both an outcome goal and a process. It is a process that will increase your natural abilities, and create attractor fields that will help you to achieve all of your outcome goals that are aligned with the big picture.

While you may not be able to control the outcome, you can control your thoughts and actions required to improve the process. Success in doing and mastering the process builds confidence and improves your brain's chemistry, making it easier to achieve your desired outcome.

If you pay the price required to master your tape and the process, it is only a matter of time until you reach your outcome goals. You can only fail if you stop trying. Use your setbacks as opportunities to learn from the feedback and to increase your desire to improve. Motivate yourself to work harder and smarter until you reach the outcome you are striving for.

This applies to being able to live the **Eight Words** 100% of the time. If you're not able to be always truthful, become more truthful. If you're not able to be always positive, become more positive. If you're not able to always be helpful, become more helpful. If you keep striving to do your best to always live the **Eight Words**, it is just a matter of time until you will be able to.

Setting goals and writing them down are very important steps on the road to success. However, most individuals do not have goals. If they do, they usually fail to write them down. Written goals have, what seems to be, a mysterious way of becoming real as I explained in Chapter 6: Cause and Effect -- Attractor Fields.

There are two reasons why people don't write down goals. The first reason is similar to why many people stop making New Year Resolutions. They do not keep their resolutions or goals; so they stop making them. The second reason why individuals do not write down their goals is that it is time consuming. Also, their goals may change and have to be rewritten.

A short cut for keeping written goals is to use 3 by 5 index cards. (You can buy 100 of them for about a dollar.) Take a stack of index cards and write down each thing you desire to happen in your life (short, medium and long-term goals) on a separate index card. Then, put them in order of importance to you. Do not be concerned with what you consider is realistic or unrealistic to accomplish. Just write it down and place it in its order of importance. As your goals change, toss out the cards that no longer apply and add new ones. Then, rearrange the cards in their order of priority. This method for keeping written goals is easy. It saves you a lot of time.

I recommend reading your cards at least twice a day; once at night before you go to sleep and once in the morning when you get up. If you do, you will be amazed how many of your dreams come true. Sometimes it may take months or years for your goals to materialize. However, if you do this on a regular basis, you will be way ahead of the game. The goal cards keep you and your tape on course by reminding you where to focus your energy to attain your desires. Don't forget to write down the process goals needed to accomplish your outcome goals.

In Chapter 3: Self-Awareness and "The Eight Words", I recommended that you print out the "**The Eight Words**" page and put it in a nice frame where you will see it frequently every day like I do. The more times that you reflect upon these **Eight Words** through out the day, the easier it will become to live your life by them without making any exceptions.

Performance over Time

Rarely do individuals improve or change overnight. Normally, performance improves over time in a gradual up and down progression as your learn from the feedback how to keep getting better. By constantly aligning your thoughts and actions with the **Eight Words**, you will gain the strength and ability to master your tape and the processes that lead to reaching your goals.

The amount of time required to reach your outcome goals depends on the strength of your desire and the action you take. It can be a fast journey or a slow one. You set your pace according to your desire and action.

I hope you realize that desire without action is just a wish. A wish is not strong enough to change your tape and your life.

Improve Your Brain's Chemistry by Changing Your Tape

In Chapter 2: Owner's Manual for Human Beings, I explained how to improve your brain's chemistry by changing what is on your tape. I strongly recommend that you reread this chapter several times until you completely understand how your chemistry and tape affect your entire life.

If you have a strong desire to increase your success and happiness, make living the **Eight Words** a major part of your life because this is the *fastest way* to change your tape and improve your brain's chemistry. If you do, you will increase all of your natural abilities and make your life a lot smoother and happier.

Thoughts: Facts and Emotions

Your thoughts from outside stimuli have two components: facts and emotions. Every stimulus you receive through your nervous system is nothing more than a fact. However, you attach emotions to these facts and they are recorded on your tape. Whenever a similar situation or fact recurs, your tape automatically plays back the previously recorded emotional response.

Your emotional response is acceptable if the emotions are positive. However, negative emotions (big or small) cause adverse chemical secretions that literally poison your brain's ability to function. Once you comprehend the profound influence negative emotions have on your brain's chemistry, you can become much more objective and less emotionally involved with the facts in your life.

Start restructuring your negative emotional attachments to certain facts recorded on your tape. Facts are merely facts! However, you can choose your emotional response to them. Learn to accept the facts you can't change and change the facts you can with a positive attitude.

Anytime you have any degree of love, generosity, praise and bravery or multiple combinations of these emotions, your brain secretes positive chemicals and enhances your natural abilities to change the facts to what you desire.

As I mentioned before, it is a lot easier to be always truthful than to be always positive. To become always positive it is imperative that you are at least always truthful, especially to yourself.

Otherwise, the negative emotions on your tape will rule your life because they will lower your chemistry and diminish your ability to reason. You will continue to rationalize why you are justified for allowing negative emotions to remain on your tape and influence your thoughts and actions to your detriment as well as to the detriment of those around you.

In the process of becoming always truthful, you will remove many of the negative emotions that motivate you to lie. Once you are honest with the outside world and yourself, the next step is to start reducing and eventually eliminating all the negative emotions on your tape that you have associated with certain facts in your life.

While you may not be able to control the facts, fair or unfair, you encounter in your life, you can choose how to respond emotionally to these facts. Anytime you have any degree of hate, greed, jealousy, and fear or multiple combinations of these emotions, you are lowering your brain's chemistry and hurting yourself.

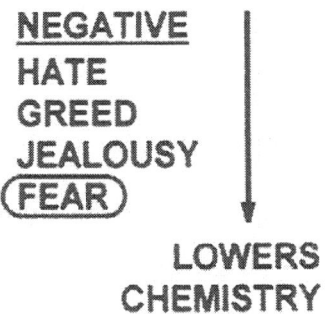

NEGATIVE
HATE
GREED
JEALOUSY
(FEAR)

LOWERS
CHEMISTRY

Since I have helped thousands of athletes to increase their performance by showing them how to reduce and eliminate fear and anger from their tapes, let me share some insights that can help you to do the same.

Fear

> *"Fear defeats more people than any other one thing*
> *in the world" -Ralph Waldo Emerson*

Fear normally leads the list of negative emotions in all sports and life in general. Yet, fear is the easiest negative emotion to overcome if you are objective and understand its source. It can be fear of failure, making a mistake, losing your job, spouse, health, life or the countless other fears you may have.

Fear can manifest itself as a strong emotion, causing you to hyperventilate and your knees to shake. It can create stress and ruin your health. Fear can be a weaker emotion and cause you to be indecisive and keep you from taking action. Anytime you allow fear to enter your emotions, whether it is strong or weak, your judgment and natural abilities suffer.

Reducing fear and eventually eliminating it is easier if you know why it exists and what to do about it. The first step is to clearly understand that the emotion of fear adversely affects the chemistry of your brain and all of your natural abilities. Next, realize your thoughts have two components: facts and emotions. Every situation you face in your life is nothing more than a fact. Facts are merely facts! It is the fear you have attached to certain facts that allows fear to exist, not the facts.

Stop reading and write down all of your fears on a piece of paper. It is important that you are honest with yourself and take the time right now to list your fears.

I have fears about or I'm afraid of:

1) _____
2) _____
3) _____
4) _____
5) _____

After you have written down all of your fears, take a look at the facts that you have attached your fears to.

Without seeing the list you have written down, all the facts that you have attached fear to have one thing in common. They are all *potential outcomes* that have *not yet* occurred. Once you clearly understand that you are afraid of something that has not happened, you are on your way to reducing or eliminating your fears.

On reflection you'll realize fear is always associated with concern over a future outcome *before* it even occurs. ***Fear cannot exist in the present***. *Stop and let this sink in!* It is only when you are concerned about a future outcome that fear can exist.

Since you can only physically exist in the present, you only have control of the present. How well you control the present determines the future outcome -- good or bad. Once you clearly understand that your fear about a future outcome contributes to your downfall by lowering your chemistry and reducing your ability to function at your best, it becomes easier to face and handle your fear. The only way to successfully overcome fear is to stay in the present. Focus on what you can do in the present moment and let the outcome take care of itself – win or lose.

Fears are based on imagined scenarios that may or may not happen. Most imagined fears never happen. The following are some quotes to illustrate this point:

"The only thing we have to fear is fear itself"
~ Franklin D. Roosevelt

"Fears are nothing more than states of mind"
~ Napoleon Hill

"When I look back on all these worries, I remember the story
of the old man who said on his deathbed that he had had a
lot of trouble in his life, most of which had never happened."
~ Winston Churchill

*"If you see 10 troubles coming down the road, you can be
sure that 9 will run into the ditch before they reach you."*
~ Calvin Coolidge

*"We are more often frightened than hurt; and we suffer
more from imagination than from reality."*
~ Seneca

*"Cowardice ... is almost always simply a lack of ability
to suspend the functioning of the imagination."*
~ Ernest Hemingway

*"How many feasible projects have miscarried through despondency,
and have been strangled in their birth by a cowardly imagination."*
~ Jeremy Collier

*"Cowards die many times before their deaths;
The valiant never taste of death but once."*
~ William Shakespeare

*"Don't be afraid your life will end;
be afraid it will never begin."*
~ Grace Hansen

*"If you listen to your fears, you will die never knowing
what a great person you might have been."*
~ Robert Schuller

*"You can conquer almost any fear if you will only make up
your mind to do so. For remember, fear doesn't exist
anywhere except in the mind."*
-Dale Carnegie

Since fear can only exist in your mind when you are concerned
about a future outcome, separate the facts that you have fears attached
to into two types: one by future outcomes that you have some degree

of control over; and, the other by future outcomes that are out of your direct control.

When I swam from Alcatraz to San Francisco, some people that knew about it would ask me if I was ever afraid. To me there were only three facts to be afraid of. They were: not making it to shore; drowning; and, being attacked by a shark.

Since I had a very high degree of control over the outcome of the first two facts, fear about these potential outcomes was very easy to keep from entering into my imagination. Not making it from Alcatraz to San Francisco did not cross my mind because it is not a hard swim if you are in good shape and select the right tidal conditions. The only hard part was the daily ritual of conditioning my body, mind and spirit to swim under frigid conditions. Drowning because of cramps was a very minimal concern because the swims were well supervised and they were plenty of boats close by.

The biggest fear would have been the embarrassment of having to get into a boat in front of my peers because I wasn't strong enough to finish the swim. That fear never existed because I always knew that I was strong enough to finish before I ever jumped into the water. I was in excellent physical condition and in total control of the outcome.

However, the fear of being attacked by a shark is a horse of a different color. The facts are that there are sharks in the San Francisco Bay and a swimmer in the bay was attacked by a shark in the past. However, the odds of that happening are very minimal unless it just happened to be your unlucky day. You can't control that, so why worry about it ☺.

Since the risks were very minimal and the personal rewards were great, I willingly jumped into the cold water and swam. It has been many years since I made the Alcatraz and Golden Gate Bridge swims, but I still remember how wonderful it made me feel. I literally glowed all over after those swims. It still makes me feel good inside knowing that I did something few others have accomplished.

Before you jump into the water, you have total control over the fact of being attacked by a shark. Once you jump into the water, you are at the mercy of your imagination and God or the attractor fields your mind creates.

From my own personal experience I can tell you that it is a very eerie feeling when you are half a mile from shore and you start having fears about being attacked by a shark. If you dwell on it long enough, it can paralyze you and make you want to stop swimming so the sharks won't notice you. However, you can't stop swimming until you reach shore because you will drown or die from hypothermia since the water is so cold.

The only way to eliminate the fear of sharks is to never get in the water or stop thinking about being attacked by a shark, especially while you are in the middle of a swim and really don't have a choice. While training to get into shape, there were many times I swam without a boat being nearby or even in sight. I was totally on my own without any help from sharks; or, frigid water, cramps, high waves and the strong currents in the San Francisco Bay.

Fortunately, I was a strong swimmer at that time and rarely thought about being attacked by a shark while I was swimming. When these fears entered my mind, I eliminated them by changing my focus from being concerned about the future outcome of a shark attack that only existed in my mind or imagination to one that I chose.

I chose to surround myself with a white light for protection from sharks and swim in peace without fear. If you don't know what the white light is, raise your chemistry and you will experience it yourself. The white light is a positive energy that can guide and protect you.

There are many fears you can create in your imagination if you choose to. In the wilderness where I use to live, there are herds of deer. Sometimes they run in front of cars. When I drove my car at night, I used the white light to keep the deer and myself out of harms way. You might laugh at this, but I know from experience that the white light works if you use it. It can even help athletes play in the zone once they optimize their chemistry.

By merely changing your focus, you can immediately transform your negative emotions into neutral or positive ones, depending upon what you choose to focus on. Since fear can only exist when you are imagining a future outcome, change your focus and stop dwelling on your fears.

You can focus on the present task at hand, protection or help from God or a Higher Power in the form of a white light, or you can clear your mind of all thoughts by not thinking and allowing your subconscious to act on instinct. All it takes is training until changing your focus becomes second nature or instinctive.

Once you train your mind or tape to focus solely on the present or whatever you choose, fear will no longer have a reason to exist in your life. Since the only thing that you can control is the present and your thoughts, why allow your imagined fears about the future to lower your chemistry and take away from your natural abilities?

Any time you are involved with a future outcome, there are probabilities of success and failure. Your thought selection affects your chemistry, which changes these probabilities and potential outcomes.

"A pessimist sees the difficulty in every opportunity;
an optimist sees the opportunity in every difficulty."
~ Winston Churchill

To increase your chemistry and probability of success, you must focus totally on being successful *if everything goes right.* No one is a fortune-teller and you don't know what is going to happen. However, you raise your chemistry and increase your probability of success if you are totally positive and have faith that everything will go right.

You have the power to choose what you want to focus on. Even if the odds are a million to one against you, train yourself to focus solely on the one chance of being successful. If you allow any imagined fears or doubts about the future outcome to creep into your thoughts, you lower your chemistry and dramatically increase your probability of failure.

Of course, you won't be successful all of the time. However, if you are brave and willingly accept the risk, learn from the valuable feedback that your mistakes provide, and keep trying until you succeed, you will live a much fuller and happier life.

Take a lesson from the great inventor Thomas Edison, who didn't have any formal education or scientific training. In the process of discovering how to make an incandescent light bulb work, he made over ten thousand experiments that failed. He learned from his numerous mistakes, never gave up and the rest is history. It is obvious that Edison had little or no fear of failure. So why should you?

Fear is the easiest negative emotion to reduce and eventually eliminate, if you train your mind to stop thinking about the future outcome, do the best you can do and learn from your mistakes. I have been blessed with an optimistic spirit that has known very little fear. While I have taken a lot of risks and made many mistakes in my life, I have learned much in the process.

Here is another personal experience about fear that you can learn from. After a friendly game that I won while playing with a stranger, he told me that I had intimidated him. Then he sternly said, **"I don't get intimidated."**

I asked him why he got intimidated. He replied that my level of confidence never changed whether I made or missed a shot, and I always played as if I would make the shot. Then I asked him what he did. He told me that he coached wrestling and was the lead man for a swat team.

Being curious, I asked him what exactly does the lead man for a swat team do. He told me that he was the first person through the door, and his job was to take out whoever was on the right side of the hallway or room before he was shot or killed.

I told him that I was a mental trainer and asked him how he mentally prepares himself to do his job. He told me that it's the same for wrestling or being the first one through the door. Training, training, training was his answer.

He trains himself to focus totally on executing the process without any fear or concern about the outcome. I asked him if he had any fear. He said his only fear was that his partner, the next man through the door behind him, wouldn't take out whoever was on the left side of the hallway or room.

Then he told me that he relies on his partner's training to keep him out of harms way. Can you rely on your mental or spiritual training to keep you out of harms way, or do you get emotionally involved and have fears about the outcome?

Scientific research has revealed that human beings learn and remember what they have learned through repetition. Isn't it amazing then, that so many individuals expect to read a book one time and retain it forever? It takes time and effort to get rid of your fears as well as your other negative emotions.

I call it "polishing your wheel." You have to keep polishing your wheel if you want it to shine and keep shining.

You may think my constant reference to living the **Eight Words** 100% of the time is somewhat repetitious, but that's OK. It is designed to be repetitious to encourage you to make living them a major goal in your life. Once you decide to use the **Eight Words** to guide your thoughts and actions, it's important to keep repeating and reflecting on them over and over and over again until you live your life that way without any exceptions.

> *"To know what is right and not to do it*
> *is the worst cowardice."*
> *~ Confucius*

Hate, Anger or Irritations

Just like fear, hate comes in many degrees. Intense hate causes individuals to kill and nations to go to war. It can manifest itself in lesser degrees, such as anger, or mild irritations. Since hate is a strong word and you may avoid relating to it, anger is substituted for hate in this section.

Anger is harder to eliminate than fear because it is usually much more intense, appears in a flash and tends to stay with you. As a result, your chemistry falls farther and faster than with fear. Anger's extreme negative chemical reaction throws off your ability to reason clearly, distorts your judgment, and may lead to bizarre behavior. Plus, anger tends to linger because you dwell on it far longer than fear. Fear more readily disappears once you get past your concern about a future outcome, and return to the present.

Some of you have tapes with very little anger while others are full of rage, and explode at the drop of a hat. In either case, your anger affects your judgment and ability to reason. If you get angry, fast and furious, you have a lot of work ahead of you unless you are extremely determined and self-disciplined. However, by training your tape you can greatly reduce your anger and shorten its duration if you try hard enough. It is just a matter of desire, awareness, time and effort.

It is *imperative* to totally and completely understand that negative emotions are poison. They destroy your chemistry and cause havoc with your performance, judgment and health. If you do not comprehend that anger causes unhappiness, you will allow it to continue.

If you are thirsty and I give you a glass of gasoline, would you drink it? Of course, you wouldn't. You wouldn't even think twice about drinking it. So why allow a fact, fair or unfair, upset you and rob you of the ability to reason and function at your full potential while handling that fact?

> *"For every minute you are angry*
> *you lose sixty seconds of happiness."*
> *~ Ralph Waldo Emerson*

> *"Whatever is began in anger,*
> *ends in shame."*
> *~ Benjamin Franklin*

> *"There was never an angry man*
> *that thought his anger unjust."*
> *~ St. Francis De Sales*

> *"Whenever you are angry, be assured that it is not only*
> *a present evil, but that you have increased habit."*
> *~ Epictetus*

Stop reading and write down all of the things that you hate, get you angry or irritated on a piece of paper. It is important that you are honest with yourself and take the time right now to list what angers or irritates you as well as things that you hate.

Take a minute and write down what you hate. It's important to become aware of the negative emotions that are controlling you.

I hate or get anger at or get irritated by:

1) _____
2) _____
3) _____
4) _____
5) _____

Take a look at what you have just written down. Whatever you have listed, they all have one thing in common. They are all facts that you react negatively to. While you may not be able to change the facts, you can change your negative emotional response to them if you choose to.

Any time you encounter a fact that you prefer not to have in your life, three possible situations exist. One, you can leave the situation and remove yourself from the fact. Two, you can change the situation and fact to one that you prefer. Three, you are stuck in the situation and have to deal with the fact.

No matter what facts you are stuck with or encounter in your life, you always have the choice of how you respond emotionally. It takes a very strong person not to hate or get angry at unjust actions or behavior. However, hate begets hate and anger begets anger. If you respond to an injustice with hate or anger, you are adding fuel to the fire. Why do you think mankind is in a continual state of war? Is it because of love or hate?

> *"We shall require a substantially new manner*
> *of thinking if mankind is to survive."*
> *~ Albert Einstein*

"Problems cannot be solved at the same level
of awareness that created them."
~ Albert Einstein

You may not be able to control the facts around you, but you can control your emotional response to them. A positive attitude is a great asset since it increases your brain's chemistry and creativity to help you find a solution to your situation.

Convert your anger into determination. Then work harder and smarter to change the facts into positives or accept them for what they are if you can't change them. Always look for the best, no matter how adverse your situation may seem. My philosophy is "If it does not kill you, it makes you stronger by overcoming it and the negative emotions on your tape."

Living by the **Eight Words** is not for weaklings, brooders and pouters. It is for individuals who want to be great and fly with the eagles. Anger and the desire for revenge is not a show of strength and character. It is a lack of self-control. You are better off without anger. If my straightforwardness upsets you, look for the truth in my message. Learn to get rid of your hate, anger, and petty irritations. Otherwise, your tape will have you repeat them over and over again.

Since I have been doing my best to live by the **Eight Words** for many years, let me share some of my experiences as to how I transform negative emotions of hate, anger, and irritations into positive emotions.

I have to admit that the longer I live by the **Eight Words**, the easier it becomes to remain positive and take the high road. After a while, it becomes hard to be negative or remain negative no matter what facts I encounter. It just takes training, training, and more training until you can become that way.

Whenever an injustice happens to me or in the world, I realize that ignorance was the cause. Then, I pray for the person or those that perpetrated the injustice. The two quotes below help me to keep my emotions on the high road, instead of stooping to the level of those that caused the injustice.

"Father, forgive them, for they know not what they do."
~ Jesus Christ (while hanging on the cross)

"A good man is a bad man's teacher,
and a bad man is a good man's job."
~ Lao Tzu

Since the world's injustices are not going to be solved by more injustices in the belief that the end will justify the means, I realized that the solution lies in improving my emotions and encouraging **you** and millions more to do the same. Since you can't solve a problem with the same mindset that created it, hopefully our combined efforts will eventually make this world a better place for those that will follow us when we are long gone.

I very rarely get angry any more. When I do, I immediately notice the chemical changes in my body and just let the anger go. I don't suppress the anger. I acknowledge the fact that I reacted negatively to and consciously choose to release my anger. Why be angry? It's bad for your health and makes you do things that you regret doing once you have calmed down.

Here is a game plan for reducing and eliminating your anger. First, as soon as you notice you are angry, stop and acknowledge that you are angry. Do not suppress your anger, or it will build and fester. After acknowledging you are angry, realize that you are merely reacting to a fact and *have a choice of how to respond.* You can continue to be upset or you can decide to release your anger.

Here is an excellent method for releasing anger. Take ten deep breaths and slowly exhale after each breath. This will relax you and calm you down. Then, make a big smile and talk to your tape. Tell it that you refuse to let a fact get you upset no matter how unfair or unjust the fact may be. Facts are merely facts! You may not be able to control the facts, but you can control your emotional response to them.

The more times that you consciously release your anger, the easier it becomes. After a while, you will start laughing at the things that use to get you angry.

If I ever run across an angry person that wants to vent on me or argue, I just smile and let them vent. It takes two to tango, and two angry people to fight or argue. Since I don't respond with anger, I know the angry person will eventually calm down. Once that happens, I have a civil conversation and discuss the facts that they were angry about. Sometimes we end up being friends.

Realize that there are three sides to every argument or disagreement. They are: your side, their side and the truth. Instead of defending my side, I look for the truth behind the facts and what I may have done or not have done to cause the problem. Even if I'm only at fault 1%, I'll take responsibility for my actions and do my best to correct them. Many of your personal confrontations and our world's challenges could be solved with a similar approach.

I no longer have things in my life that I hate to do. I divide my life into things that I prefer to do and prefer not to do. Most of the things in my life I love doing. When I have to do things that I prefer not to, I do it with a smile knowing that even the Buddha chopped wood and carried water.

I use these opportunities to master my tape and raise my chemistry. The more my chemistry and understanding rises, I'm finding out that there are fewer things I prefer not to do. It makes me happy when I cross off tasks that I finish from my daily to do list, especially the ones I prefer not doing and have to do.

When I find something that angers or irritates me, it makes me smile because I found another fact on my tape that I can change my negative response into a positive one and increase my chemistry in the process. *I am more concerned about changing my negative emotional reactions into positive ones, than the facts -- fair or unfair -- that I encounter in my life.* You will become that way too if you start reflecting on the **Eight Words** throughout the day.

If you are working to eliminate anger from your tape, do not become discouraged or get mad at yourself when you respond to facts with anger. Remember, your tape wants you to repeat your past and will not give up without a fight. Be patient. Be determined. Stick to your game plan.

Before going to sleep, talk to your tape. Tell it how you want to respond in the future to the facts that upset you during the day. After a while, your tape will help you in your battle to change your emotional response to facts as you become less angry, and your anger lasts for shorter periods of time.

Some individuals feel that their anger fuels their determination. However, can you always quickly transform your anger into determination? If you can, why wait to get angry before you become determined?

This may seem like a Pollyanna or unnatural way to go through life, but it sure beats going though life being angry and unhappy. Try it, you'll like it.

Greed

Greed, as defined by Webster, is excessive or reprehensible acquisitiveness.

"Greed is a bottomless pit which exhausts the person
in an endless effort to satisfy the need
without ever reaching satisfaction."
~ Erich Fromm

"The avarice person is ever in want;
let your desired aim have a fixed limit"
~ Horace

There is nothing wrong about acquiring money, possessions and things to make your life more comfortable as long as you don't lie or become selfish in the process. The best way to make a lot of money is to provide an honest product or service that helps others.

"Men are rich only as they give.
He who gives great service gets great rewards."
~ Elbert Hubbard

If you would take, you must first give,
This is the beginning of intelligence."
~ Lao Tzu

"For it is in giving that we receive."
~ St. Francis of Assisi

The best way to keep greed from clouding your judgment is to dedicate your life to helping others and spend less time thinking about yourself. If you do, you will live a very rich and happy life.

'The most satisfying thing in life is to have been able
to give a large part of oneself to others."
~ Pierre Teilhard de Chardin

"It is not what we get. But who we become,
what we contribute ... that gives meaning to our lives."
~ Anthony Robbins

"For of those to whom much is given,
much is required."
~ John F. Kennedy

Jealousy

Jealousy results when you desire something that another person possesses and you can't have or you resent them for having what you want.

"The disease of jealousy is so malignant
that it converts all it takes into its own nourishment."
~ Joseph Addison

"The jealous are possessed by a mad devil
and a dull spirit at the same time."
~ Johann Kaspar Lavater

"My wife's jealousy is getting ridiculous. The other day
she looked at my calendar and wanted to know who May was."
~ Rodney Dangerfield

I hope you enjoyed Rodney's joke ☺. All joking aside, jealousy can only exist when you are looking outside of yourself for happiness. You came into this world alone and without possessions. When you leave this world, you can't take anyone or anything with you, except your spirit.

I don't know what will happen to my spirit when it's time to leave this world. However, my gut feelings tell me that I will move on to another dimension, higher or lower, depending upon the character I developed while I was here on Mother Earth. Some people refer to it as *"heaven or hell."*

Since I can't take any possessions or things with me when it's time to move on, why be jealous of what others have. The only thing that I'll take with me is my spirit. So I'm spending my time here helping others and developing my character by doing my best to live the **Eight Words** 100% of the time.

I firmly believe the more truthful, positive and helpful to others that I become, the higher I will move up the ladder when it's my time to move on. Hopefully, you will feel as I do and make living the **Eight Words** one of your methods to climb up the ladder as high as you can before it's your time to move on. I'm positive that living by the **Eight Words** will enhance whatever religious beliefs you may have.

Wouldn't our world be a better place if everyone else felt the same way? Why be jealous of people or things, when all you have that really matters is your character and how well you treat others?

If you have faith in your own abilities and understand the big picture of life, you can achieve what you want through your own efforts and God's help.

Anytime you have any degree of love, generosity, praise, bravery or multiple combinations of these emotions, your brain secretes positive chemicals, which enhance your natural ability and happiness.

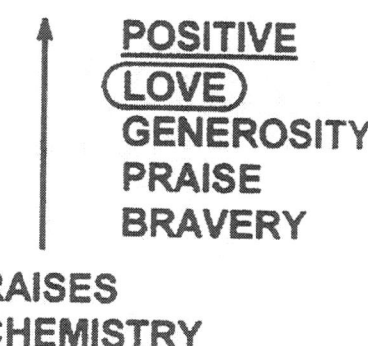

Love is the strongest positive emotion. Love is what drives individuals to noble deeds. Love allows the spirit to push on against incredible odds, hardships and obstacles. Always love your fellow human beings and have compassion, in spite of the frustrations you encounter.

There is a huge difference between loving what you do and liking what you do. Love creates a passion within you that cannot be denied. Love overcomes the option of quitting when times get tough.

If you want to be happy and successful, find what you love to do and do it with all your heart and soul. Success and happiness will follow!

Generosity is liberality in spirit, acts and giving. To me the best time of the year is Christmas or the Holiday Season because during this brief time of the year, the masses of society observe the spirit of giving and forgiving. It is a great time to be alive.

Why limit your generosity and kindness only to the Christmas or Holiday Season when you can do it every day of the year?

Praise is expressing a favorable judgment to or approval of another. When someone does something well, let them know. When someone fails, praise them for their efforts and encourage them never to give up striving to reach their dream.

Bravery allows you to face and overcome your fears. Bravery gives you the faith and courage to continue your quest against all odds.

I don't spend much time elaborating on or explaining how to be positive because just as the light of the day follows the darkness of the night, if you live by the eight words you will naturally become more positive. If you focus on becoming always truthful, releasing your negative emotions, and spending more time helping others, you will automatically become more positive and much happier.

Learn to live in the present and keep improving the process until you achieve your desired outcomes. It takes extreme bravery and faith to commit yourself totally to a journey where there are no guarantees that you will reach your destination. You must be brave and have supreme confidence in yourself to always be truthful, positive and helping others without exceptions. If you do, a meaningful life full of joy and happiness will be yours.

Since the proof is in the pudding, all you have to do is reflect on your life and your level of happiness to know that what I'm sharing with you makes total sense.

Don't just take my word for it. Prove it to yourself by doing your best to live the **Eight Words** 100% of the time and watch how much happier you become as a result.

"How To Be Happy and Have Fun Changing the World"

Chapter 8

Transforming Emotions

Positive emotions elevate your chemistry. This allows your natural talents and abilities to increase. The more skilled you become at transforming your negative emotions into positive ones in regard to the same fact, the happier you will become.

Everything you experience in your life is merely a fact. It is the negative emotions you attach to those facts that keep you from reaching your goals and being happy.

For example, getting up at 5:30 AM to exercise is a fact. If you hate getting up early, guess what happens to your chemistry and motivation to get out of bed when your alarm goes off? It is important to focus on the personal satisfaction you will receive if you do get up and exercise, instead of focusing on hating to get up. Focus on your desire to be in shape and to be in control of your tape.

The technique of transforming your emotional association to facts is done by changing your focus. When you go through life, it is much easier if you focus on the positive, instead of the negative. Here are some personal experiences from my life that may help you to understand how to do it.

When I swam in the San Francisco Bay, the water temperature would fall as winter approached. To jump into the bay during the winter months, I had to train my tape how to feel emotionally as the water got colder and colder. When the water temperature dropped to 54 degrees, I told my tape that I was about to enjoy an ecstatic experience. When the water temperature dropped below 48 degrees, I told myself that I was about to experience a state of euphoria.

When you jump into water that is 48 degrees or colder, you experience a burning sensation on your skin. You do not know if it is hot or cold, *it just burns*. Then, you hyperventilate for about a minute until you catch your breath. It can be a horrible or wonderful emotional experience depending upon what you choose to experience. I chose the latter – to make it a wonderful experience.

You may be thinking to yourself that you could care less about swimming in freezing water. But, how would you feel knowing that you swam the Golden Gate Bridge and swam from Alcatraz to San Francisco? You would probably feel very good about yourself knowing that you have a strong spirit and that you are in control, instead of your emotions.

So what does this have to do with your life? What I am doing is teaching you the process of transforming your emotional reactions to facts by showing you some extreme examples of how it is done.

During 1983-84 I worked with a swimmer, who had won two silver medals for swimming in the 1976 Olympics. He introduced me to the facts of *pain and fatigue* that he confronted while preparing for a comeback at the 1984 Olympics. The United States had boycotted the 1980 Olympics.

He told me that when he was pushing himself to swim faster, he would sometimes *hate* the pain he experienced as his lungs burned for oxygen. There were other times when he would hold back from pushing himself faster because he *feared* the pain he would suffer.

I explained to him that until the body adapts itself to increased work loads, you experience pain and fatigue. Pain and fatigue are nothing more than facts. It is your choice how you wish to emotionally experience them. If you attach hate or fear to the pain and fatigue, guess what happens to your chemistry and your ability to push your body faster?

Creating positive emotions of love and bravery allow you to push on in spite of your discomfort. Positive emotions cause your brain to secrete chemicals that block out the pain and give you additional energy. For example, the "runner's high" is created by individuals pushing themselves beyond the wall of pain and fatigue until their brains secrete endorphins, a biochemical with properties similar to morphine. Athletes love and become addicted to this high.

If you find yourself in situations that approach your pain and fatigue thresholds, consciously realize that pain and fatigue are facts. *You can choose how you want to experience them emotionally.* Instead of hating or fearing pain and fatigue, focus all your attention on the pleasure you receive from controlling your tape. Love knowing that you control your destiny and are on your way to becoming the best of the best. Happiness and success are the rewards for pushing yourself beyond what others are willing to do.

The swimmer that I was mentally training related very well to this concept. Unfortunately, he missed making the 1984 Olympic team by less than a few hundredths of a second. After he did not make the Olympic team, he apologized for not taking my program more seriously in other parts of his life. He told me that he had allowed certain personal factors in his life to hold him back. It is important to realize that your emotional state affects your entire life and everything that you do.

Now that you have some extreme examples of how to transform your emotions to facts, I will apply this technique to your life. Train yourself to transform all your negative emotional reactions into positive ones by changing your focus. It is a challenge to always remain positive. It can be accomplished with effort *over time* as you train your tape to respond with positive emotions, instead of negative ones.

You can transform your negative emotions into positive ones by creating a mind set that your glass is always half full. You don't want to go through life with a glass that is half empty. The liquid is in the middle of the glass, but there can be two different emotions to the same fact. One is positive and one is negative. It is up to you to decide if your glass is half full or half empty.

If you believe that your glass is half full, you will have a higher level of chemistry then if you believe that your glass is half empty. As simple as this concept sounds, it can make the difference between living a happy life or an unhappy one. The nice thing about it is that it's your choice and totally in your control.

Remember, every situation in your life is nothing more than a fact! While you may not be able to control the facts, you can control your emotional response to them. If you do, you will have more fun and be more successful.

All it takes is a conscious effort to realize that any negative emotional response you have to any fact, *fair or unfair*, poisons your chemistry and hinders your natural abilities. Once you completely understand that negative emotions in any degree contribute to your unhappiness and failures, you can start transforming the negative emotions on your tape into positive ones by simply changing your focus. It is done by working at it, over and over, until it becomes an instinctive habit.

Learn from your mistakes and make the appropriate adjustments. Become the master of your tape and your emotions. Love life and accept all of its challenges. Be brave and determined to succeed in spite of all odds or hardships.

The Olympics is the most respected and widely watched sporting event in the world. The Gold Medal is a symbol of mankind's highest level of achievement in the world of sports. It is the reward for years of personal sacrifice and self-discipline.

Olympic athletes are very dedicated and focused individuals. They work very hard to perfect themselves and their performance. They cannot afford to have any negative emotions, and not do their very best because it will cost them their dreams. Are you doing your best to achieve your dreams?

To master your tape and transfer your negative emotions into positive ones requires the same constant effort of an Olympic athlete. However, it can be accomplished. All it takes is a strong desire and persistent action on your part to live the **Eight Words** 100% of the time.

"He who conquers himself is the mightiest warrior."
~ Confucius

"How To Be Happy and Have Fun Changing the World"

Chapter 9

Have Fun Helping to Change the World

*"Little progress can be made by merely attempting to repress
what is evil. Our great hope lies in developing what is good."
~ Calvin Coolidge*

*"To put the world in order, we must first put the nation in order;
to put the nation in order, we must put the family in order;
to put the family in order, we must cultivate our
personal life; and to cultivate our personal life,
we must first set our hearts right."
~ Confucius*

*"The more man meditates upon good thoughts, the better will
be his world and the world at large."
~ Confucius*

*"If you think in terms of a year, plant a seed;
if in terms of ten years, plant trees;
if in terms of 100 years, teach the people."
~ Confucius*

*"Sincerity and truth are the basis of every virtue."
~ Confucius*

*"I Am Always Truthful, Positive, And Helping Others"
~ Michael Anthony*

Need I say more? If enough individuals were always truthful, positive and helping others, would it change the world we live in? ***You know it would.***

The only possibility that this will happen depends on ***you*** and millions of others like you. If you want to have fun helping to change the world, start with yourself by doing your best to live the **Eight Words** 100% of the time, and recommend others to read my book and do the same.

I'm sure that everyone at some time in his or her life was taught to be truthful, positive, and to help others. However, there is a huge difference between knowing what to do, and actually doing it without exceptions. Olympic athletes win Gold Medals not by knowing what to do. They win them because they practice doing the right things over and over and over again until it becomes a part of them.

This same principle applies to you and everyone else. It's not what you know. It's what you do that counts and makes a difference in your life. Knowing the **Eight Words** is one thing, but saying and living them over and over and over again will make them a part of your life. Your life will become a positive example for others to follow. They will feel your energy, and want to feel the same way.

The same holds true when you teach or learn. The things that are stressed and repeated over and over again are remembered. What you teach or learn once is quickly forgotten. Do you still remember the alphabet and the time tables that were taught to you in grade school? Do you remember how much repetition it took you to learn them until you knew them by heart?

Since the teacher always learns more than the student, the more ***you*** share the **Eight Words** with others and discuss it with them, the more aware and happier you will become. The **Eight Words** are simple to understand, but will have a profound influence on your life and everyone that you share them with. They have the power to change the world once they gain a critical mass. *You* are invited to live them 100% and help make our world a better place.

If you want to live the **Eight Words** and encourage others to do the same, the following are some ways you can help. I'm sure that you will come up with many more ideas on your own as you become more creative.

Parents

If you have young children, what better gift can you give them then teaching them to be always truthful, positive and helping others in their formative years? Children are the future leaders of our world. The values you teach them will greatly impact their lives and many others.

When you put your children to bed at night, repeat the **Eight Words** out loud with them. Spend some time discussing how their day was in relation to these **Eight Words**. If you keep it simple, they will understand what you are teaching them and remember it when they leave home and enter the world.

If you have teenagers, read this book together with them. Make it a point to sit down with them every day or as often as possible and follow the same steps above. Be open and honest with them and they will eventually be the same with you. They are young and have to make their own mistakes, but at least help them to keep their mistakes small.

If your children have left home, share this book with them. Then watch how much closer they will become to you as your conversations become more open and meaningful, especially if they are raising children of their own.

If you have grand children, make sure you teach them the **Eight Words** in case their parents don't.

Married Couples and Domestic Partners

Read this book together with your spouse or partner. Since we are all individuals, we have different interest and priorities. Fair compromises and kept agreements are the key to all successful relationships. Living by the **Eight Words** is a great foundation for all relationships to build upon.

Don't forget to tell your friends and associates to read this book. Then have fun discussing it with them.

Individuals

Tell your family, friends and associates to read this book. Then have fun discussing it with them. Since everyone has different strengths and weaknesses on their tapes, you can help each other to increase your awareness and happiness by living the **Eight Words** and sharing your experiences.

Teachers, Professors and Principals

Where appropriate, teach the **Eight Words** and the insights in this book to your students. If possible, tell their parents about this book.

If you truly understand the value of the **Eight Words**, use your imagination and help make this book a part of your school or university's curriculum.

Coaches

Young and mature athletes relate very well to the insights in this book. Study this book and use it to help them to focus on improving the process and allow the outcome to take care of itself. Recommend that they read this book as well. Winning is merely the by-product of doing the process better than your competition. Part of the process is to develop a great mental game by learning to control your emotions and to play on instinct.

Living the **Eight Words** will keep both you and your team honest. An honest person knows his weaknesses and works to improve them. You will find that my book, *The Mental Keys to Improve Your Golf* is easier to use and applicable to all sports if you change the golf facts to the facts of your sport when you read this book.

12 Step Programs

If you are a member of a 12 Step Program, tell your members about this book. It will inspire them and reinforce you program.

> *"You will never find an honest addict."*
> *~ Margie (a recovering addict)*

Corporate CEOs and Business Owners

It's one thing to have a mission statement and code of ethics; it's another thing to live by them. If you relate well to the **Eight Words**, make it a part of your business culture.

To make the **Eight Words** a part of your business culture, place copies of it on the walls of your business and on your desks. Recommend that your employees reflect upon it at least once a day, and conduct their affairs with your business accordingly. Encourage them to read *How To Be Happy*.

Give your customers and prospects a copy of the **Eight Words**. Tell them that this is how you run your business. Feel free to include the **Eight Words** in your advertising and marketing campaigns.

Employees

Give a copy of the **Eight Words** to your manager, boss or owner of where you are employed and tell them about this book. If you can't live by the **Eight Words** where you work, find another job where you can or start your own business.

Citizens of the United States of America

The founders of the United States of America wrote our great Constitution and the Bill of Rights to protect our inalienable rights of Life, Liberty and the pursuit of Happiness. Contrary to popular opinion, we are a republic and the government is the servant of the people.

Many of our elected government officials and judges are not keeping their solemn oath to uphold the laws of our great Constitution. Many make their solemn oath and then conveniently forget about it. Why are we allowing our government officials to feel and act as if the people are the servants of the government, instead of the other way around?

If you want to protect your rights and liberty, email all of your elected representatives and the judges who interpret the law and tell them to read this book. Plus, print out a copy of **Eight Words** and mail it to them. Make them accountable by insisting that they keep their solemn oaths to uphold the laws of our Constitution and Bill of Rights, as well as their campaign promises. When they don't, take a minute to send them an email and put them on notice. If enough of us keep doing this, our elected representatives will eventually get the message and act accordingly.

> *"If you ever injected truth into politics,*
> *you would have no politics."*
> *~ Will Rogers*

104

*"Anyone who doesn't take truth seriously in small matters
cannot be trusted in large ones either."*
~ *Albert Einstein*

The United States of America is a great country with many individual rights, freedoms and privileges. Let's keep it that way by standing up for the rights God gave us and are protected by our Constitution and Bill of Rights.

Citizens of the World

We are all citizens of the same world. We must learn to love each other and forgive the injustices that we inflict on each other. Injustices can be met with force and cause more hatred and injustices. Or, injustices can be met with the power of the truth and compassion to see both sides of the issue and deal with them fairly for all concerned.

If our present world leaders won't deal with the issues while always being truthful, positive and helping others, hopefully our children or their children will do so when it's their turn to lead the world. However, if we don't teach our children to live by the **Eight Words** 100% of the time, the world and its injustices will never change.

*"Insanity is doing the same thing over and over again
and expecting different results."*
~ *Albert Einstein*

Many governments rule their citizens by fear. When the citizens no longer have fear, the government loses its power to control by fear and intimidation. Eliminate fear from your life and encourage your fellow country men and women to do the same. If you can't be brave, teach your children to live by the **Eight Words** when they are young so they can be brave and defend their inalienable rights of life, liberty and the pursuit of happiness when they grow up.

World Leaders

If you are in charge or control of a country and its policies, you are in a position of power to do many great things. Do your country and the world a major favor by living the **Eight Words** 100% of the time and leading your country accordingly.

When you make decisions, forget yourself and your special interest groups. Do the right thing, and be fair to all sides of the issue.

Talk Show Hosts

If you have a favorite talk show hosts, tell them about this book and recommend that they have me appear on their show. If you are a talk show host or its producer, read this book and invite me on your show for an interview. You and your audience's spirits will be uplifted by the message in this book.

Website Owners

Tell your visitors about "How To Be Happy." If you have an email newsletter or blog, make a special announcement to your subscribers recommending that they read this book.

Post Reviews and Comments on Social Media and Amazon

LIKE my Facebook/HowToBeHappy page and share it with your friends. Tweet your friends and followers about my happy book.

Post a review or your positive comments about this book on Amazon and the other major book distributors.

Parting Message

I can't reach the critical mass needed to change the values of our society by myself. Your help is needed to share the **Eight Words** with others.

If the message of this book has struck a chord with you, live the **Eight Words** to the best of your ability, and tell your family, friends, and associates to read this book. If you do, you will have fun helping to change our world for our children and their children's children.

I have to admit that is has been a lot of fun writing this book. I, also, have to admit that I had to overcome some fears and reservations in baring my soul and feelings with you. At one point my spirit told me to stop thinking and just write. When I heard this, I had a good laugh at myself and decided to write whatever my spirit came up with.

Hopefully, you liked what my spirit wrote and have decided to make living the **Eight Words** 100% of the time a major goal in your life as well as encouraging your family, friends, and associates to do the same. If you do, you will live a very happy life and help make our world a much better place for those that follow in our footsteps.

God Bless you,

Michael Anthony Klosek

FYI

Michael Klosek is my birth name.
Anthony is my confirmation name.
Michael Anthony is my spirit's name.

P.S. I did my job. I hope you will do yours and help out.

"The Eight Words"

I

AM

ALWAYS

TRUTHFUL,

POSITIVE,

AND

HELPING

OTHERS

Printed in Great Britain
by Amazon.co.uk, Ltd.,
Marston Gate.